DIMENSIONS
OF
GRACE

KOJO OWUSU-ANSAH

ISBN: 978-9988-2-1456-2

Kojo Owusu-Ansah
P.O. Box BT 535
Tema
Tel: +233(0) 545 309 992
E-mail: kowusuansah@gmail.com
Twitter: @kojo_owusuansah
Instagram: Kojo_owusuansah
Facebook: www.facebook.com/kojo.owusuansah.7
website: www.kojoowusuansah.org

Editing by Samilia N. T. Dodoo
Email: samiliad@yahoo.com
Mobile: +233 20 024 6954

Designed and Printed by
Kobina Eshun
Email: kobina.eshun@gmail.com
Mobile: +233 20 833 5437

Other book by the author:
The Right Foundation

Contents

DEDICATION

I dedicate this book to my dear mother Mary Mina-Ama Akpe.
You have fought on every side and have come out victoriously.
Your love and passion for the house of God has gained expression in your
children.
The grace on your life is so great.
Mum, I love you and God richly bless you.

ACKNOWLEDGEMENT

My utmost gratitude goes to God for granting me the grace to come out with yet another book. Your grace towards me is extravagant. I love you LORD!

My sincere appreciation also goes to the founder and visionary of Miracle Life Gospel Church, Rev. Dr. & Rev Mrs. Kisseih. Your ministry has impacted my life greatly.

I am indebted to the man whose ministry has transformed and shaped my life for the past three years. Your timely messages were what inspired me to publish this book. **Daddy Evans Darko-Mensah** you are richly blessed. Thank you for investing in me.

I also acknowledge Rev. Dr. Kwasi Boateng, Rev. Theodore Quarcoopome, Rev. Jacob Zotbah, Pastor Eric Tenkorang and Pastor Ross Bulley for contributing to my spiritual growth.

I am also grateful to the CEO of CIS Ghana Mr. Saqib Nazir, for giving me the opportunity to gain work experience in the corporate world.

My thanks also go to the poet, Maxine Gloria Danso who featured a poem on each chapter.

To my wonderful parents Mr. & Mrs. Akpe, Mr. Christian Owusu-Ansah, the Ackon family, and my siblings; Comfort, Yaw, Sarah, Ama, Setor, Ato and Enyo, you are a blessing to be with.

To my church, Miracle Life Gospel Church (Faith Chapel) family, I'm grateful for your love and encouragement.

To my buddy, friend, brother and personal assistant, Charles Amanor, you are such a blessing. Words alone cannot express my loads of gratitude to you. Walking with you has been such a great delight. Chasey, you are blessed!!!

INTRODUCTION

Does grace have dimensions? According to Ephesians 3:18 love has dimensions, because it is high, low, deep and wide. It is important to know that grace is a subset of love and in as much as love has dimensions, grace also has dimensions.

According to Collins English Dictionary, *dimension* is the measurement of the size of something in a particular direction, such as the length, width, height, or diameter.

God is love (1John 4:8) and God in the flesh was full of grace and truth (John 1:14). Therefore, love was in the flesh and love was full of grace and truth. Therefore, wherever love goes, grace also goes with it.

In this book, you'll see the extent to which grace reaches in various aspects of our lives. They are too numerous to contain in this book. I believe through the few areas I have shared in this book, the Lord will enlighten you and impact grace into you for a victorious life.

You are blessed!

FOREWORD

For me, *grace* is everything. If you search through the many English translations of the Bible you will find *Grace* exalted by a wide range of "superlatives" including *Abundant, Amazing, Bountiful, Extraordinary, Glorious, Wonderful* – to mention a few.

Grace is not a doctrine or a teaching or even a concept. Grace is a Person and His name is Jesus Christ. God, who alone is wise, has given us His best – Jesus Christ – who alone is complete to meet every need of the creation. It is therefore no wonder that the Holy Scriptures reveal the many dimensions of Grace – as Peter puts it in 1 Peter 4:10 – the **manifold** Grace of God.

An excellent job has been done in revealing how Grace is available to meet every situation – from Evangelism and Leadership through Marriage, Prayer and Spiritual Warfare and other situations. Each chapter is loaded with Scriptures that show the sufficiency of the Grace of Our Lord Jesus Christ to meet specific needs. The book is very well written and practical in application and I will not hesitate to recommend it to anyone who really wants to grow in the Grace and in the knowledge of Our Lord Jesus Christ.

Like Paul, I say to all readers *"So now, brethren, I commend you to God and to the word of His Grace, which is able to build you up and give you an inheritance among all those who are sanctified'. Acts 20:32* $_{NKJV}$.
To God be the Glory for this wonderful gift to the faithful in Christ.

Evans Darko-Mensah

MLGC, Tema

CHAPTER 1
UNDERSTANDING GRACE

Let it be defined, or even tried to be explained
Let all the wisdom be sought and knowledge gained
It still remains a complex unfathomable veracity
And a simple notion of love extended to humanity

The human life and system of living has been attributed to ones efforts, that is, what one can do or cannot do in life. For instance, certificates are awarded in the educational system to show the achievements and efforts of an individual during his schooling period. The judiciary judgmental system is based on what someone did or couldn't do. Everything about this life is centred on the individual.

"Grace is the unmerited, undeserved and unearned Favour of God by which He has given me the most PRECIOUS GIFT of His Beloved Son, Jesus Christ, to LIVE IN ME with ALL His Wisdom, Power and Glory."
Evans Darko-Mensah

Talking on the subject of grace at times is very difficult for the natural man to understand fully but I pray our Father in heaven will grant you spiritual insight and understanding as I share on this all important subject of grace.
The word *'grace'* literally means *'favour'*. In Hebrew, it is CHEN from a root word CHANAN - to bend or stoop in kindness to another as a superior to an inferior (Strong's 2603). In Greek, it is CHARIS and has the idea of graciousness in manner or action (Strong's 5485). It comes from a root word CHAIRO to be cheerful, happy (Strong's 5463). When

used in reference to God, it is the benevolent action of Him stooping down to us in His kindness to reach us in our need, and convey upon us a benefit. His grace has been termed *'unmerited favour'* but it is more than an attitude of favour or mercy. His mercy is an expression of His compassion towards us, but His grace is an extension of benevolence translated into action that releases His enabling power into our lives. Various people have also expressed their insight on the same word "Grace" to mean:

- Jesus Christ

- Unmerited or undeserved favour

- God's riches at Christ's expense

- God's real attitude clearly expressed

- A compensating factor

- A divine enablement

- Bestowal of divine gifts

Personally, I agree totally with all the above expressions on the meanings of grace. Grace is an offer God gives with the person of his son Jesus Christ. When you receive Jesus who is full of grace and truth (John 1:14) you have also received grace. Andy Stanley said, "Grace is an unmerited favour not based on our own efforts or focused on what you can do or cannot do. You can ask for grace. You can plead for grace. But the minute you begin to think you deserve it, it is no longer grace. It is something you have earned. Remember, grace can't be earned. It is the knowledge of what we do not deserve that allows us to receive grace for what it is. Unmerited. Unearned. Undeserved. For that reason, grace can be experienced by those who acknowledge they are undeserving."

Grace is not a New Testament idea. However, we see grace personified in Jesus in the New Testament. It was in operation before the creation of man. God created the world, filled it with goodness, and then gave it away. He handed us the keys. He created a world perfectly suited to sustain the human race. What did we do to deserve this incredible, pristine abundance? Nothing. Absolutely nothing!

The interesting thing to note is that, "All things were made by Jesus; and without him was not anything made that was made" (John 1:3). For by him were all things created, that are in heaven, and that are in earth, visible and invisible, whether they be thrones, or dominions, or principalities, or powers: all things were created by him, and for him: And he is before all things, and by him all things consist (Colossians 1:16-17). Therefore, grace began with Jesus. The free air, sunshine, water, etc. were all made by him. He came on earth full of that same grace and truth to show us the heart of the Father; that God still loves the world (John 3:16).

Andy Stanley in his book, 'The Grace of God' said, "Have you ever thanked God for light? Me neither, we take it for granted. We don't generally consider the creation of light as an extension of God's grace. That's grace. From the standpoint of human experience, the creation of the universe and God giving it to humanity was the beginning of grace. Majestic sunsets – those are for you. The seasons that enable us to plant and harvest – those are for you. The varieties of fruits and vegetables you have enjoyed throughout your life – those are for you. Your choice of salmon, sea bass, trout, or snapper – that's for you. The beach, the mountains, the lakes, the streams, the rainforest, the jungles, the plains – all for you. There is some beauty in this world that no one person can fully comprehend, greater abundance, than no one person can consume. Why? That's the nature of grace. Grace is never just enough. Grace is always far more than enough. From the very outset, God established his pattern of lavishing grace upon the entire world."

When God created the world the final thing the Bible said in Genesis 1:31 was, "Then God looked over all he had made and he saw that it was VERY GOOD! (*emphasis is mine*). Life, as God designed it, is to be VERY GOOD but the reflection of what we see in the world is not very good. The sickness, poverty, hardships, pain, hurt, immorality, greed, armed robbery, corruption, death and all the bad things you can think of in the world express the consequences of the fall of man.

Once upon a time, in the book of Genesis, God created everything in

3

this world including man (male and female). He prepared a garden and placed man in it giving him access to everything in the garden except to eat the fruit of one particular tree. Adam disobeyed God and that resulted in a number of consequences:

- Separation from God.

- A drive out of the VERY GOOD life God designed for them.

- Prevention of man from enjoying the perfection that God has put in creation.

- A transfer of authority (rulership, dominion, reigning mandate) to Satan thereby becoming slaves to the devil.

- A shift from the kingdom of God to the devil's kingdom.

- An activation of the wrath of God, thereby, resulting in curses on their destinies.

- They were no longer the children of God.

Romans 5:17 says, "For if by one man's offence death reigned by one; much more they which receive abundance of grace and of the gift of righteousness shall reign in life by one, Jesus Christ."

The one man in the above scripture refers to Adam. The first man, Adam, brought death into the world by committing an offense called sin and that sin brought death. Death does not only represent physical death or separation from God but it also means sickness, poverty, corruption, unforgiveness, envy, slander, shame, famine, anger, lies, murder, disappointment and many other negative things you can think of.

So Adam allowed the human race to experience death but thanks be to God that he gave humanity a second chance to enjoy that VERY GOOD life he had in mind when he created the world. The solution is for all who will receive abundance of grace and the gift of righteousness through Jesus Christ. Therefore, for you to enjoy God's abundant grace, you have to confess with your mouth the Lord Jesus, and believe in your heart that God has raised him from the dead and you shall be saved. For with the heart man believeth unto righteousness and with the mouth confession is made unto salvation (Romans 10:9-10). The moment you receive Jesus into your life, you are restored to your original position and the result becomes:

- No separation with God.

- Being brought back to the VERY GOOD life God designed for man.

- You have authority (rulership, dominion, reigning mandate) over Satan.

- A shift from the devil's kingdom to God's own kingdom.

- No wrath from God towards you and free blessings rather than curses.

- You now become a child of God.

Categories of Grace
Grace can also be categorised into three different kinds:
1. **Grace to be**; who God has made you to be.

2. **Grace to have**; what God has freely given to you.

3. **Grace to do**; what God requires of you.

Grace to Be
Paul said, "I am what I am by the grace of God" (1 Corinthians 10:15). Grace has the ability to make you what God wants you TO BE. First and foremost, you are a Christian because of grace and not only that, but grace has also made you TO BE:
- His friend (John 15:14)

- His child (1John 3:1)

- An heir (Galatians 4:7)

- Blessed with all spiritual blessings (Ephesians 1:3)

Whatever level you are in life is all because of His grace, so acknowledge God and thank him for his free gift of grace. God is not through with you yet, for the word of God says, "…the path of the just is as the shining light, that shineth more and more unto the perfect day" (Proverbs 4:18)

When grace comes, disgrace ends. You are what God says you are!

Grace to Have

We now have this light shining in our hearts, but we ourselves are like fragile clay jars containing this great treasure. This makes it clear that our great power is from God, not from ourselves (2 Corinthians 4:7).

As Christians our ability to express any talent or gift is simply because we received it from God and that excellency of power must be attributed to God and no one else. The reason why we HAVE is because of grace through Jesus Christ and not because of what we have done or our personality; for God is no respecter of persons.

It is important to know that God deals with us based on His promises.

"This letter is from Simon Peter, a slave and apostle of Jesus Christ. I am writing to you who share the same precious faith we have. This faith was given to you because of the justice and fairness of Jesus Christ, our God and Saviour. May God give you more and more grace and peace as you grow in your knowledge of God and Jesus our Lord. By his divine power, **God has given us everything we need for living a godly life.** We have received all of this by coming to know him, the one who called us to himself by means of his marvelous glory and excellence. And because of his glory and excellence, **he has given us great and precious promises.** These are the promises that enable you to share his divine nature and escape the world's corruption caused by human desires.

In view of all these, make every effort to respond to God's promises. Supplement your faith with a generous provision of moral excellence, and moral excellence with knowledge, and knowledge with self-control, and self-control with patient endurance, and patient endurance with godliness, and godliness with brotherly affection, and brotherly affection with love for everyone. The more you grow like this, the more productive and useful you will be in your knowledge of our Lord Jesus Christ. But those who fail to develop in this way are shortsighted or blind, forgetting that they have been cleansed from their old sins. So, dear brothers and sisters, work hard to prove that you really are among those God has called and chosen. Do these things and you will never fall away (2 Peter 1:1-10 NLT)".

Every condition to any promise in the Old Testament has been fulfilled by Jesus Christ with a resounding "Yes!" and through Christ our "Amen" (which means *Yes*) ascends to God for his glory (2 Corinthians 1:20). Jesus has done everything the law requires. Believing in Jesus, you can appropriate all of God's promises for your life. For he has done it and by grace you have it!

In Deuteronomy 28, God promised the children of Israel a lot of blessings that will be theirs only if they abide by the condition outlined in verse one, "If you fully obey the LORD your God and carefully keep all his commands that I am giving you today, the LORD your God will set you high above all the nations of the world."
Another instance is in Joshua 1:8 "Study this book of instruction continually. Meditate on it day and night so you will be sure to obey everything written in it. Only then will you prosper and succeed in all you do."

It is important to know that all these conditions were before the New Covenant we have in Christ Jesus. The children of Israel could not receive the blessings permanently because they could not follow through the various instructions daily. But even that, God told them to present sacrifices every time they failed in order to qualify for His blessings. Thanks be to God that Jesus fulfilled every condition attached to any blessing in the Bible (2 Corinthians 2:20). When we believe in Him, therefore, we qualify to receive those blessings.
Your ability to have God's blessings is simply through your belief in what Jesus has done on the cross for you. His finished works give you access to God's blessings. Believe in Him to access God's blessings of what has been freely given to us.

Grace to have is also expressed through our walk with the Holy Spirit.

Now we have received, not the spirit of the world, but the spirit which is of God; that we might know the things that are freely given to us of God (1 Corinthians 2:12). When we acknowledge the Holy Spirit and walk with him, we'll gain knowledge of all the free gifts in the Lord and have them.

The sunshine, air, nature, variety of fishes, etc. have all been given to us freely. Grace to have, does not depend on you but what God has freely provided for us.

Grace to Do

"For by grace you have been saved through faith, and that not of yourselves; it is the gift of God, not of works, lest anyone should boast. For we are His workmanship, created in Christ Jesus for good works, which God prepared beforehand that we should walk in them." Ephesians 2:8-10 NKJV

After salvation, God requires us to do certain good works he has planned long time ago and He helps us do it by his own grace. What are these good works and what has it got to do with grace? Does it mean if I don't have grace I can't do them?

For the first part of the question, good works are good services and things we do in life. For instance, giving to the poor and needy, building of schools and hospitals, serving in church and any other good thing you can think of to impact society positively. Grace has a role in good works in that, "no one can receive anything unless God gives it from heaven" John 3:27 NLT. Therefore, since the money, strength, and wisdom to do the good works come from God then it has to do with grace. Now tell me, what is it that you have done that God should give you strength, wisdom, skills or any other capability? None of us deserve anything from God. He gives us because he loves us (John 3:16). The enablement from grace makes our effort successful and better than if we had done it without grace. Grace enables us to get a lasting result of the things we do than without God's grace.

Paul laboured more abundantly than they all yet it was not him at work but God's grace that was at work in him (1 Corinthians 15:10). He said in Galatians 2:20 that, "I am crucified with Christ: nevertheless I live; yet not I, but Christ liveth in me: and the life which I now live in the flesh I live by the faith of the Son of God, who loved me and gave himself for me. Also in Colossians 1:26-27, "Even the mystery which had been hid from ages and from generations, but now is made manifest to his saints: To whom God would make known what is the riches of the glory of this mystery among the Gentiles; which is Christ in you, the hope of glory". Paul emphasised that it is Christ who was at work in him and this is a mystery which he unfolded to the Gentiles. This secret is for you and me to take full advantage of: CHRIST IN ME, THE HOPE OF GLORY.

Any situation you come across which is too great or difficult to handle, know that Jesus Christ is living in you. Be conscious of this truth and allow Jesus Christ to work on that task, situation or circumstance for you. He is your wisdom, strength, knowledge, understanding and every good thing.

My manager at work called me to his office one day and gave me a task to perform. I had four days for completion and submission. It wasn't an easy task for me. I nearly said no but I remembered with Christ at work in me, I can do all things. I took the challenge and the Lord caused all grace to abound towards me. To the glory of God, I was able to finish and submit before the deadline. Yet not I, but Christ at work in me.

Scripture says we are labourers together with God (1 Corinthians 3:9) and faith without works is dead (James 2:26). This clearly shows our efforts are necessary in the Kingdom of God and the Lord also makes his grace available for us.

Excerpts from Grace

Tony Cooke in his book the "DNA of God" outlines these excerpts about grace:

- The Lord is gracious (Psalm 111:4).

- He is the giver of grace (Proverbs 3:34).

- He is the God of all grace (1Peter 5:10).

- His throne is a throne of grace (Hebrews 4:16).

- Our message is called "The Gospel of the Grace of God" and "The Word of His Grace" (Acts 20:24, 32).

- The prophet of old prophesied of the grace that should come to us (1 Peter 1:10). This grace came by Jesus (John 1:17).

- Jesus was full of grace, and it is from His fullness that we receive one grace after another (John 1:14, 16).

- The grace of God was upon Jesus and gracious words proceeded out of His mouth (Luke 2:40; 4:22).

- It was by grace that Jesus tasted of death for every man (Hebrews 2:9).

We are told to:
- Continue in grace (Acts 13:43).

- Abound in grace (2 Corinthians 8:7).

- Be strong in grace (2 Timothy 2:1).

- Grow in grace (2 Peter 3:18).

The Word of God speaks of:
- Great grace (Acts 4:33).

- The abundance of grace (Romans 5:17).

- The exceeding grace of God (2 Corinthians 9:14).

- The glory of His grace (Ephesians 1:6).

- The riches of His grace (Ephesians 3:7).

- The grace of life (1 Peter 3:7).

- The manifold grace of God (1 Peter 4:10).

- The true grace of God (1 Peter 5:12).

Grace can be:
- Found (Genesis 6:8; Hebrews 4:16).

- Shown (Ezra 9:8).

- Poured (Psalm 45:2).

- Received (Romans 1:5).

- Seen and perceived (Acts 11:23; Galatians 2:9).

Grace saves us and empowers us to live a life pleasing to God:
- We are saved by grace and through grace (Acts 15:11; Ephesians 2:8).

- It is through the grace of God that we believe (Acts 18:27).

- Grace builds us up and gives us an inheritance (Acts 20:32).

- We are justified freely by his grace (Romans 3:24).

- Grace makes the promise sure to all those who have faith (Romans 4:16).

- Paul ministered through the grace that was given to him (Romans 12:3).

- We have gifts differing according to the grace that is given to us (Romans 12:6).

- Grace causes us to be enriched by Him in all utterance and in all knowledge (1 Corinthians 1:4-5).

- Grace makes us what we are and works in us and through us (1 Corinthians 15:10).

- It is the grace of God that makes us rich (2 Corinthians 8:9)

- God's grace is sufficient for us and causes us to reign in life (2 Corinthians 12:9; Romans 5:17).

- We are called by grace into grace (Galatians 1:6, 15).

- Grace causes us to preach the unsearchable riches of Christ

(Ephesians 3:8)

- Our words can impart grace to others (Ephesians 4:29).

- We are partakers of grace (Philippians 1:7).

- We sing with grace in our hearts, and our words are to be seasoned with grace (Colossians 3:16; 4:6).

- Grace gives us everlasting consolation and good hope (2 Thessalonians 2:16).

- Grace teaches us to live holy lives (Titus 2:11-12).

- Grace helps us in time of need (Hebrews 4:16).

- Grace enables us to serve God acceptably (Hebrews 12:28).

- Grace establishes our hearts (Hebrews 13:9).

- Grace is obtained by coming boldly before His throne (Hebrews 4:16).

- Grace is multiplied unto us through the knowledge of God and of Jesus our Lord (2 Peter 1:2).

An individual can:
- Receive grace in vain (2 Corinthians 6:1).

- Set aside or treat as meaningless the grace of God (Galatians 2:21).

- Fall from grace (Galatians 5:4).

- Insult the Spirit of grace (Hebrews 10:29).

- Fall short of grace (Hebrews 12:15).

- Turn the grace of God into lewdness (Jude 4).

CHAPTER 2
GRACE FOR EVANGELISM

From every corner, let it be heard aloud
That we may gather from afar, a mighty crowd
Let us speak and shout and proclaim for all to know
The glory of God; for we have been strengthened for so

Research done by Peter Wagner indicates that only about 10 percent of Christians see themselves as effective evangelists.
Have you wondered why whenever there is a call to evangelism only a few people come around and go to witness? Or perhaps you are part of those who absent themselves and so don't even know what I'm talking about?

Evangelism is what I will say has become our greatest attitudinal challenge as a church. By the inspiration of the Holy Spirit, I will define evangelism as an invitation children of God extend to a dead man – someone separated from God (Ephesians 2:1) to come and receive life or relationship or fellowship with God (Father) through Christ Jesus and to take his original place of dominion over all the earth (Ephesians 2:10).

For you to comprehend this definition, it is important to understand the whole concept of creation. Scripture makes us understand that God created the heavens and the earth (Gen 1:1) and the entire universe for his own pleasure and will or purpose. Psalm 24:1 also says, "The earth is the LORD'S, and everything in it. The world and all its people belong to him." God became a sovereign king over his creation. He then decided to make man in His own image and likeness to rule over his physical creation which is earth. Yet not man at work but then God's own Spirit at work in man.

Man who was to have dominion in the physical realm sinned against God thereby losing that dominion to Satan. The sin Adam committed was equal to high treason and the only punishment for this was death (separation from God). God therefore in his own wisdom found a way to restore man (male and female) back to his original position of dominion on earth through Christ Jesus (John 3:16, Romans 17:5).

Evangelism is to enable man gain access to his original position of dominion in the earth realm and not heaven (Psalm 115:15-16). When one becomes born again (to accept Jesus as your Lord and saviour) that person is now in a kingdom with his dominion intact to rule as God originally intended in Genesis 1:26 "And God said, Let us make man in our image, after our likeness: and let them have dominion over the fish of the sea, and over the fowl of the air, and over the cattle, and over all the earth, and over every creeping thing that creepeth upon the earth" and Psalm 115:15-16 also says, "Ye are blessed of the LORD which made heaven and earth. The heaven, even the heavens, are the LORD's: but the earth hath he given to the children of men".

I hope by now you have understood the concept of God's kingdom, his plan for man in that kingdom and what evangelism is all about.

My question is, if we, who are children of God, have been restored to our rightful place in creation through Christ Jesus, why has it become an attitudinal challenge to most of us to go out and call the lost children of God to come in and enjoy the benefits and blessings in the Kingdom of God?

I like the way one servant of God puts it; the church is the educational institution of the Kingdom of heaven and is here to affect, enforce, propagate and preach the gospel of the Kingdom to the world.

Why are some churches indifferent in fulfilling their divine calling? Why then do some of us come to church with a mindset that evangelism or propagating the gospel of the Kingdom is for some selected few or a section of the church? I strongly believe that this settled way of thinking has affected majority of God's children.

God makes grace available for evangelism. Jesus said, "Peace be with you. As the Father has sent me, so I am sending you" John 20:21 NLT. If Jesus is sending us in the same capacity as the Father sent him then we need not be reluctant and afraid of anything but to reach out to lost souls in the entire world. Before Jesus began his public ministry he went to the synagogue and read Isaiah 61:1 "The Spirit of the LORD is upon me, for he has anointed me to bring Good News to the poor. He has sent me to proclaim that captives will be released, that the blind will see, that the oppressed will be set free, and that the time of the LORD'S favour has come." Jesus was equipped with the Holy Spirit for ministry. The same way, Jesus equipped the disciples with the baptism of the Holy Spirit in Acts 1:8 before they reached out for souls.

"But you will receive power when the Holy Spirit comes upon you. And you will be my witnesses, telling people about me everywhere – in Jerusalem, throughout Judea, in Samaria, and to the ends of the earth." Acts1:8 NLT

Notice that Jesus said 'You will be' meaning when the Holy Spirit comes upon you, witnessing becomes your nature. You don't do evangelism but you are a witness. I call this aspect the unconscious part of evangelism. Everything about you should simply communicate Jesus to people. Your life, family, business, and anything you are involved in simply express God's goodness. When anyone asks you how come you are able to obtain such a good result in your life, family or business etc. you simply tell them it's because of Jesus. This is a good ground to tell someone about Jesus.

Before Jesus ascended on high, he told us to, "Go and make disciples of all nations, baptising them in the name of the Father and the Son and the Holy Spirit" Matthew 28:19 NLT. This is what I call the conscious side of evangelism. This is different from forcing yourself to do evangelism. What it means here is, by nature you are a witness so beware of it and go make disciples. This mindset takes away stress and self-effort in evangelism. I believe majority of the church have not really understood their new nature after the baptism of the Holy Spirit and so they remain where they are without fulfilling the great commission.

It is also important we understand that:

1. **We need to know and appreciate that soul winning is the ultimate purpose of God for mankind.**

    As I said earlier, in Gen 1:26, God's purpose has been to restore us to his original intent for creating mankind. In John 3:16 God had to come down in a form of man to save mankind from sin. Again in 1 Timothy 2:4, scripture makes us understand God wants everyone to be saved, know and understand the truth. The ultimate purpose of God for mankind is for us to be saved and that is still his ultimate purpose and the church cannot afford to think less than that.

2. **We need to maintain a right attitude towards the ultimate reality of life.**

    I like the way Myles Munroe puts it, "currently, the world's population exceeds 6 billion. China has over 1 billion people, the vast majority of whom have not heard the name of Jesus. Only 1% or less of the Chinese population are believers and followers of Christ. India's population has crossed the 1 billion thresholds. Approximately 98 percent of India is Hindu, Buddhist, or Muslim. Again, 1 percent or less believe and follow Christ. What this means is that in those two nations alone, more than 2.2 billion people do not know Christ and most of them have never heard the gospel.

    Hebrews 9:27 expresses that, "And just as each person is destined to die once and after that comes judgment" and Matthew 16:26 also says, "And what do you benefit if you gain the whole world but lose your own soul? Is anything worth more than your soul?" The soul is the most expensive thing in the whole world because the value of a thing is determined by what you give in exchange for it. "For you know that God paid a ransom to save you from the empty life you inherited from your ancestors.

And it was not paid with mere gold or silver, which lose their value. It was the precious blood of Christ, the sinless, spotless lamb of God" 1 Peter 1:18, 19 NLT. The soul is equivalent to the blood of Jesus because it took the blood of Jesus to save our souls. Nothing in this whole universe could redeem us from the grip of Satan except the precious blood of Jesus Christ. This makes every soul important to God.

Until we live our lives with this mindset and maintain the right attitude towards the ultimate reality of life, our world will end up in hell.

3. The foundation of the word and prayer needs to be in place to make evangelism a delight.

In as much as the disciples were witnesses they never neglected the ministry of the study of God's word and prayer. "But we will give ourselves continually to prayer, and to the ministry of the word" Acts 6:4 KJV. And now, brethren, I commend you to God, and to the word of his grace, which is able to build you up, and to give you an inheritance among all them which are sanctified. Acts 20:32

But you, dear friends, must build each other up in your most holy faith, pray in the power of the Holy Spirit. Jude 1:20 NLT If the foundation of the study of God's word and prayer are in place, evangelism is always a delight.

4. Our partnership with the Holy Spirit needs to be intact.

John 15:26 says, "But I will send you the advocate - the Spirit of truth. He will come to you from the Father and will testify all about me." It is important to note that the ministry of evangelism was given to the Holy Spirit and so for us to be involved in evangelism we really need His assistance.

Jesus said, "For apart from me you can do nothing"
John 15:5 NLT and now in his place is the Holy Spirit and so

without the Holy Spirit we can do nothing. Why not rely on his grace today as you live a life of a witness. My spiritual Father in the Faith taught me to declare every day that, "By the grace of God I am a soul winner, yet not I but Christ in me".

5. Leadership must take up responsibility in the area of evangelism.

Leadership responsibility cannot be under estimated when it comes to evangelism. For instance, Jesus being the head of the church sent out his disciples to evangelise. It therefore behoves on every leader leading the church of God to send out the church to witness to the lost.

Paul encouraged Timothy to *work at telling others the Good News, and fully carry out the ministry God has given him* (2 Timothy 4:5). Leaders, encourage your followers to reach out for souls. Enlighten them on who they are in Christ and evangelism will be a delight for each and every one of them.

CHAPTER 3
GRACE (IS ABUNDANT) FOR REIGNING IN LIFE

To speak as though there were not a care
Nor a worry of what to eat, drink or even wear
For the power within that makes us reign,
Magnifies the Truth and suppresses all pain

"Death is automatic and to overcome the power of death is not automatic, it is for those who will receive."
Evans Darko-Mensah

*For if by one man's offence **death** reigned by one; much more they which receive abundance of grace and of the gift of righteousness shall reign in life by one, Jesus Christ. Romans 5:17*

It is important to note that Jesus Christ dealt with death once and for all. Death here stands for physical death, spiritual death and eternal death. Physical death means the loss of life - permanent cessation of all vital functions. God told Adam, "the day you eat of this fruit you will surely die" (Genesis 2:17) and a day is like a 1000 years in the sight of God (Psalm 90:4) and surely too Adam did not live a 1000 years but 930 years and died (Genesis 5:5).

Today physical death is reigning over all the seed of Adam because of the sin of one man. Spiritual death means a spiritual separation from God even while you are still living physically (Ephesians 2:4-6) and eternal death means to be eternally separated from God. When you die physically your spirit man will still be alive but when the spirit is separated from God, it is described as eternal death. All those who are eternally dead are doomed in hell forever (Matthew 8:12). Also, death is symbolised in the form of sickness, poverty, unemployment, indebtedness, divorce and any bad thing you can think of.

In Hebrews 2:14-18 NLT scripture says, "Because God's children are human beings — made of flesh and blood — the Son also became flesh and blood. For only as a human being could he die, and only by dying could he break the power of the devil, who had the power of death. Only in this way could he set free all who have lived their lives as slaves to the fear of dying. We also know that the Son did not come to help angels; he came to help the descendants of Abraham. Therefore, it was necessary for him to be made in every respect like us, his brothers and sisters, so that he could be our merciful and faithful High Priest before God. Then he could offer a sacrifice that would take away the sins of the people. Since he himself has gone through suffering and testing, he is able to help us when we are being tested."

You will note that Christ through death destroyed death and the one who had the power of death. Note that it says the one who HAD the power of death, meaning Satan does not have the power of death anymore. The root cause of death has been dealt with. Death was not just destroyed by Jesus but he destroyed the devil that was having the power of death. For instance, if you smell a bad scent in your room and choose to use an air refresher to spray the room, you'll realise that after some few minutes the smell will come back. But if you search for the root cause of the smell and extinguish it once and for all, there is no way that smell will come back again. That is what Jesus did for us. He destroyed death totally so that it will not reign over us but that we should reign over it through abundant grace and the gift of righteousness.

We also see something in Colossians 2:13-15, "You were dead because of your sins and because your sinful nature was not yet cut away. Then God made you alive with Christ, for he forgave all our sins. He cancelled the record of the charges against us and took it away by nailing it to the cross. In this way, he disarmed the spiritual rulers and authorities. He shamed them publicly by his victory over them on the cross." This scripture also emphasises the victory we have in Jesus over the devil.

Jesus has saved mankind thoroughly to the root, perfectly that we need not experience any form of death. "Wherefore he is able also to save them to the uttermost that come unto God by him, seeing he ever liveth to make intercession for them." Hebrews 7:25 KJV
It is important to know that if death is destroyed completely and we have received abundant grace and the gift of righteousness, then you have no excuse if you don't reign in life. You can reign with abundance of grace and the gift of righteousness if you only *know how to*. If you don't know how to reign, death will reign. *Why should death reign again if it has been destroyed completely?* You see, friend, the devil doesn't play by the rules and so the knowledge you have about what Jesus Christ did for you will cause you to reign. For instance, if you owed a mortgage company and a friend pays off the money for you without your knowledge you are likely to pay for it unless your friend tells you it has been paid. So the knowledge of what your friend has done will set you free. This is true of what we are saying here.

How to Reign In Life
   1. **By knowing:** To know means to have the understanding or revelatory knowledge of what Christ Jesus has done for you in every area of your life so you can reign in life through Him. It is vital that you know it for yourself and not a second-hand knowledge.

   "And there were seven sons of one Sceva, a Jew, and chief of the priests, which did so. And the evil spirit answered and said, Jesus I know, and Paul I know; but who are ye? And the man in whom the evil spirit was leaped on them, and overcame them, and prevailed against them, so that they fled out of that house naked and wounded" Acts 19:14-16.
   The sons of Sceva were simply disgraced because they based on second-hand knowledge. To know what Christ has done for you in every area of your life is the first step to reign because

Dimensions of grace - Kojo Owusu-Ansah

the knowledge of the truth is what will set you free in order to soar higher in life.

For instance, if you are poor scripture says in 2 Corinthians 8:9 that, "For we know the grace of our Lord Jesus Christ, that, though he was rich, yet for your sakes he became poor, that ye through his poverty might be rich. Psalm 35:27 also says "...Let the LORD be magnified, which has pleasure in the prosperity of his servant." Jesus delights in blessing you. It is his good pleasure to see you blessed in every area of your life.

Also, if you are sick, the word of God says, *"Who his own self bare our sins in his own body on the tree, that we, being dead to sins, should live unto righteousness: by whose stripes ye were healed."* *1Peter 2:24.* By the stripes of Jesus you are healed. Your knowledge in the finished work of Jesus Christ covering any problem or challenge is the first point of your ability to reign. The Bible makes us know that we have been given the Spirit of God so we can know the things which have been freely given to us (1 Corinthians 2:12). God has also blessed us with every spiritual blessing in the heavenly places because we are united with Christ (Ephesians 1:3). Do you know every physical thing you see came from the spirit realm? Everything physical that you see and admire and call it a blessing also has a spiritual version. That's why God went to all the places in heaven, where divine health is located, marriage, children, cars, real estates, precious minerals like gold and took all these blessings in the heavenly realms and blessed you with it. Allow the Holy Spirit to help you find them in His word and that is the first process of reigning in life.

Another area of knowing is to know for a truth that Jesus lives in you. That awareness - I cannot, Jesus you can do it is very important to overcome any challenge in life. Everything that you face, ask the Jesus in you to do it. Jesus lives in you (Colossians 1:27) in all his wisdom, knowledge, understanding, power, etc. Ask Jesus in you to express his nature through you in all your endeavours and that will cause you to reign in life.

2. **By Believing**: After you know what Christ has done, you have to believe in them. Have a firm conviction, confidence and boldness in what you know. Wrong belief is worse than wrong action. Your belief determines what you say and do.

3. **By Confessing**: Your ability to know only does not guarantee the victory you want to see that has already been won by Jesus on the cross. You have to engage the truth or knowledge in confession. Hebrews 4:14 says "Seeing then that we have a great high priest, that is passed into the heavens, Jesus the Son of God, let us hold fast our profession." Hold on to your confession because Jesus holds it before the Father. Many times we don't get the confessions we make because we give up easily or change what we have said (Ecclesiastes 5:6).

    Confessing God's word against any form of death (sickness, poverty, bondage, fear, etc.) from an understanding heart guarantees the victory you want to see that has already been won on the cross of Jesus Christ. Anytime you confess God's word he watches over that word to perform because it confirms what he has done or said (Jeremiah 1:12).

    Confession is an act of Faith. "We having the same spirit of faith, according as it is written, I believed, and therefore have I spoken; we also believe, and therefore speak" 2 Corinthians 4:13. It is of faith that it might be according to grace. Faith without action is dead. You confessing, saying or declaring is the action and it will produce the desired result you want.

    It is important to note that in the realms of the spirit everything begins with words. God spoke the world into existence and we have been made in his image and likeness. When the storm rose against Jesus and the disciples, Jesus had to rebuke the storm. He spoke against the negative situation. From now begin to declare your freedom, peace, wholeness, deliverance and the entire salvation package in Christ Jesus.

Mark 11:23 says, "I tell you the truth, you can say to this mountain, 'May you be lifted up and thrown into the sea,' and it will happen. But you must really believe that it will happen and have no doubt in your heart." The removal of every mountain (obstacle, hindrance, liability, demonic attacks, etc.) is by saying and so is the receiving of every blessing also by saying. Confession brings your possession.

4. **By Prayer**: Prayer is a communication with God in the name of Jesus. Prayer causes us to reign in life. The first thought that needs to come to mind anytime you come before God should be Jesus. Our faith should be in Jesus to receive anything from God. This is because; Jesus says so in His word. John 15:16 NLT, "You didn't choose me. I chose you. I appointed you to go and produce lasting fruit, so that the Father will give you whatever you ask for, using my name."

Also, because he has a covenant with the Father on our behalf. Hebrews 8:10-12 NLT "But this is the new covenant I will make with the people of Israel on that day, says the Lord: I will put my laws in their minds, and I will write them on their hearts. I will be their God, and they will be my people. And they will not need to teach their neighbours, nor will they need to teach their relatives, saying, 'You should know the Lord.' For everyone, from the least to the greatest, will know me already. And I will forgive their wickedness, and I will never again remember their sins."

Furthermore, because Jesus has opened the way to the Father Romans 3:23, 24 NLT "For everyone has sinned; we all fall short of God's glorious standard. Yet God freely and graciously declares that we are righteous. He did this through Christ Jesus when he freed us from the penalty for our sins". Lastly, because Jesus has paid for everything. John 3:16 NLT "For this is how God loved the world: He gave his one and only Son, so that everyone who believes in him will not perish but have eternal life."

Prayer is one of the greatest weapons a believer has in Christ. The believer who prays takes commanding heights over any situation that comes his or her way. If you refuse to pray nothing will happen but prayer causes you to reign in life. E.M Bounds said, "Prayer moves the hand of God to cause things to happen on earth." It is vital to understand prayer to enjoy its maximum benefits to enable you reign in life. There are various forms of prayer that one can engage in. They include prayer of agreement, prayer of petition, prayer of praise, worship and thanksgiving, prayer of faith, prayer of consecration and prayer of supplication. In a jiffy, let me expound a little on the various forms of prayer.

- Prayer of Agreement:

  Matthew 18:19 NLT "I also tell you this: If two of you agree here on earth concerning anything you ask, my Father in heaven will do it for you." With this form of prayer you have to agree with a partner, probably your spouse to pray. If both of you are praying for a car but one is requesting a BMW and the other VW then your prayer is not in agreement and will not be answered. Both of you have to decide on one thing and ask God for it in Jesus' name.

- Prayer of Faith/Petition:

  Mark 11:23, 24 NLT "I tell you the truth, you can say to this mountain, 'May you be lifted up and thrown into the sea,' and it will happen. But you must really believe it will happen and have no doubt in your heart. I tell you, you can pray for anything, and if you believe that you've received it, it will be yours." This form of prayer has to do with praying the promises of God. After you pray you must believe that it is answered and you have the results. Nothing should cause you to doubt God. For instance, if you are sick and you pray according to 1 Peter 2:24 that by the stripes of Jesus I am healed and later doubt your healing then it is no longer a prayer of Faith.

- Prayer of Praise, Worship & Thanksgiving:

Luke 18:43 NLT "Instantly the man could see, and he followed Jesus, praising God. And all who saw it praised God, too." Philippians 4:6 also says, "Don't worry about anything; instead, pray about everything. Tell God what you need, and thank him for all he has done." This is the only prayer that can be directed to Jesus.

Andrew Wommack shared something worth hearing in his September 2014 Newsletter: Paul and Silas' praise released God's power. You see, Praise to God blesses you, drives away the devil, and blesses God. When you find yourself in an adverse situation and you offer genuine praises to God, you put yourself in a position to receive from him! Praise is the key that unlocks God's treasures.

Bishop David Oyedepo also outlined these benefits to his church during the month of August 2014 based on that month's theme of Praise.

- Praise, among others; provokes the flow of revelation 2 Kings 3:15-18/ Isaiah 30:29-30 / 60:1-22

- Provokes intervention – 2 Corinthians 20:22-24/ Psalm 47:5-7

- Provokes divine multiplication - Jeremiah 30:19-20/ John 6:5-11

- Provokes divine guidance - Isaiah 30:19-21/ Psalm 100:4 / 16:11

- Brings supernatural promotion - Habakkuk 3:17-19

- Provokes divine health - Psalm 100:4/ 84:7

- Provokes divine favour - Psalm 119:164/ 30:5-7

- Provokes supernatural blessings - Psalm 67:5-7/

Joel 1:11-12

- Provokes divine vengeance - Psalm 149:3-7/ 2 Samuel 6:14-23

- Empowers our access to realms of signs and wonders - Exodus15:11

- Facilitates the fulfillment of the prophecies – 2 Corinthians 20:14-24/ 1 Timothy 1:18

- Prayer of Intercession:

Ephesians 1:15-18 NLT "Ever since I first heard of your strong faith in the Lord Jesus and your love for God's people everywhere, I have not stopped thanking God for you. I pray for you constantly, asking God, the glorious Father of our Lord Jesus Christ, to give you spiritual wisdom and insight so that you might grow in your knowledge of God. I pray that your hearts will be flooded with light so that you can understand the confident hope he has given to those he called – his holy people who are his rich and glorious inheritance."

Romans 8:26, 27 NLT
"And the Holy Spirit helps us in our weakness. For example, we don't know what God wants us to pray for. But the Holy Spirit prays for us with groanings that cannot be expressed in words. And the Father who knows all hearts knows what the Spirit is saying, for the Spirit pleads for us believers in harmony with God's own will."

Prayer of intercession is acting in prayer on behalf of someone. The best form of intercession is to pray in tongues because the Father who knows all hearts knows what the Spirit is saying. At times you are likely to pray for a friend's financial breakthrough but actually the friend needs a job. Also, there are times you may have a deep feeling on your heart to pray for someone. You don't know what is wrong with him or her but praying in tongues will convey the right message to the Father since it is the Holy Spirit at work.

- Prayer of Consecration & Dedication:

  Luke 22:41, 42 NLT "He walked away, about a stone's throw, and knelt down and prayed, 'Father, if you are willing, please take this cup of suffering away from me. Yet I want your will to be done, not mine'."

  Isaiah 48:17 NLT "This is what the Lord says - your Redeemer, the Holy One of Israel: "I am the Lord your God, who teaches you what is good for you and leads you along the paths you should follow."

  Psalm 32:8 NLT "The Lord says, "I will guide you along the best pathway for your life. I will advise you and watch over you."

  This form of prayer is when you have to decide between two good things and don't know which way to turn to. Jesus had to pray this prayer in the garden of Gethsemane for God's will to be done in His life. You and I have to pray God's will in our lives as well.

- Prayer of Binding & Loosing:

  Matthew 18:18 NLT "I tell you the truth, whatever you forbid on earth will be forbidden in heaven, and whatever you permit on earth will be permitted in heaven."

  Binding and loosing should be based on the authority God has granted you in scripture not on some desire you have.

5. **By Resting**: Resting causes you to reign in life. It is a Holy Spirit directed activity. It is about receiving from Jesus His peace, His grace and His wisdom. It is allowing the Holy Spirit

to lead us to do the right things at the right time, with the most amazing God-kind of results. By so doing one is not worried, impatient or fearful because his or her life is directed and led by the Holy Spirit. When the Holy Spirit leads you, your life will be full of victories.

To rest is to have confidence, patience and believe in what God has said in His word. God is God and He will definitely bring to pass what He has said concerning you. When you rest, Jesus will cause you to receive His inexhaustible grace, wisdom and supply. You can rest. The work is finished. Jesus has provided everything you'll ever need!

Let's look at what the Bible says in Hebrews 4:1-11 NLT. "God's promise of entering his rest still stands, so we ought to tremble with fear that some of you might fail to experience it. For this good news—that God has prepared this rest—has been announced to us just as it was to them. But it did them no good because they didn't share the faith of those who listened to God. For only we who believe can enter his rest. As for the others, God said, "In my anger I took an oath: 'They will never enter my place of rest,' even though this rest has been ready since he made the world. We know it is ready because of the place in the Scriptures where it mentions the seventh day: "On the seventh day God rested from all his work." But in the other passage God said, "They will never enter my place of rest."

So God's rest is there for people to enter, but those who first heard this good news failed to enter because they disobeyed God. So God set another time for entering his rest, and that time is today. God announced this through David much later in the words already quoted: "Today when you hear his voice, don't harden your hearts."

Now if Joshua had succeeded in giving them this rest, God would not have spoken about another day of rest still to come. So there is a special rest still waiting for the people of God. For all who have entered into God's rest have rested from their labours, just as God did after creating the world. So let us do our best to enter that rest. But if we disobey God, as the people of Israel did, we will fall."

The scripture quoted is talking about the rest of God. I like the part which says, "God has set another time for entering his rest, and that time is today". Today, choose to rest in the Lord. The rest comes about by believing in all that Jesus has done for you. 1 Corinthians 2:12 says, "And we have received God's Spirit (not the world's spirit), so we can know the wonderful things God has freely given us." That Holy Spirit will show you all that Jesus has done for you. Spend time in His presence and in His word. Believe everything He shows you and choose to rest in Him. Rest in his divine health, prosperity, deliverance, redemption, salvation, forgiveness, righteousness, peace, honour, glory, riches, favour and all the good things in Christ Jesus today.

When Jesus was about to feed the 5000 people not counting women and children, he told the disciples to group them and to let them sit. Why did Jesus tell them to sit? The supplies came when they obeyed and sat down (rested) though they had not seen the loaves and fishes yet. Your expectations will not be delayed, God has said it and he is not a man that should lie. Rest in his promises. Scripture says, "Rest in the LORD, and wait patiently for him…" Psalm 37:7. Trust in Him wholly and rest in Him today. Rest causes you to reign in life.

6. **By Loving**: Love summarises all the commandments of God. When you show love to your enemies you reign over them. Givers are rulers. When you love, you give (John 3:16). When you give; adversaries are tamed, evil people repent, distant people become friends, wayward children are won, marriages thrive, families flourish, armed robbers are disarmed, communities live in harmony and nations prosper. You can save a lot of time spent in prayers against evil people if you'll care to show them love. Love causes you to reign in life.

CHAPTER 4
GRACE FOR FINANCIAL ABUNDANCE

The widows to care for and the orphans to feed
The love and resources to provide for all in need
The joy in knowing you can be kind and care
Just because there is a blessing to do good and share

The grace of our Lord Jesus Christ leads to financial abundance. It comes by putting your faith in the finished works of Jesus Christ. When one journeys through the bible, there are a number of things that are required of man **to do** in order to enjoy the blessings of God; but our faith and trust in Jesus Christ qualifies us to enjoy the blessings of God.

For instance, in Deuteronomy 28:1-14 if you are not able to follow through in verse 1 then forget all the blessings that are in the subsequent verses. There is no way man can fully follow through all of God's commandments, but thanks be to God, that Jesus Christ followed through and obeyed all of God's commandments for us. In 2 Corinthians 1:20 Bible says, "For all the promises of God in Him are yes and in Him are Amen, to the glory of God through us." This means every condition attached to any blessing has been fulfilled in Christ that is why in Him the promises of God are 'Yes' and in Him they are 'Amen'. If you put your trust and faith in Jesus Christ you'll enjoy every promise of God.

Some examples of God's grace for abundant blessings through the Bible:
- Exodus 11:1-3 NLT

"Then the Lord said to Moses, "I will strike Pharaoh and the land of Egypt with one more blow. After that, Pharaoh will let you leave this country. In fact, he will be so eager to get rid of you that he will force you all to leave. Tell all the Israelite men and women to ask their Egyptian neighbours for articles of silver and gold." (Now the Lord had caused the Egyptians to look favourably on the people of Israel. And Moses was considered a very great man in the land of Egypt, respected by Pharaoh's officials and the Egyptian people alike.)"

The favour (grace) God gave the Israelites made them rich. At that time the law was not given. They relied on God and not their self-effort and that made them rich. I would like you to know that the favour of God is upon your life to enrich you abundantly (only if you are in Christ Jesus by being born again).

- Isaiah 45:3 NLT

"And I will give you treasures hidden in the darkness – secret riches. I will do this so you may know that I am the Lord, the God of Israel, the one who calls you by name."

The secret riches here have nothing to do with man's effort but God's own grace.

- Job 27:16, 17 NLT

"Evil people may have piles of money and may store away mounds of clothing. But the righteous will wear that clothing, and the innocent will divide that money."

Today it is Jesus who makes us righteous (2 Corinthians 5:21) and not by our own physical doings and therefore qualifies us to enjoy silver we didn't labour for. This also applies to Proverbs 13:22 which says, "A good man leaves an inheritance to his children's children, But the wealth of the sinner is stored up for the righteous."

- Psalm 68:19

  Blessed be the Lord, who daily loadeth us with benefits, even the God of our salvation. Selah."

The Lord loads us with benefits each and every day. The benefits come in the form of his favour, love, protection, provision, deliverance, wholeness, wellness, guidance, wisdom and many other good things. Rely on Jesus for more and more of his benefits daily.

- Proverbs 10:22 NLT

  "The blessing of the Lord makes a person rich, and he adds no sorrow with it."

We have been blessed with all spiritual blessing because we are united with Christ (Ephesians 1:3) and therefore we are rich.

- John 10:10 NLT

  "The thief's purpose is to steal and kill and destroy. My purpose is to give them a rich and satisfying life."

The ultimate purpose of Jesus is to give us abundant life: rich and satisfying life. If you are in Jesus, thank God for this opportunity of an abundant life.

- 2 Corinthians 9:8

  "And God is able to make all grace abound toward you; that ye, always having all sufficiency in all things, may abound to every good work:"

The grace of God enriches our lives. Appropriate the grace of God to enjoy all sufficiency in life.

Understanding Tithes and Offerings

Tithes and offerings have become one of the most debatable topics in the church today. There are those who see tithes as part of the law and therefore not relevant for our times now. Others have made it become a stumbling block not to attend church services because they'll have to give their tithes and offerings. Many others point accusing fingers at pastors as enjoying people's tithes and offerings and for that matter they are tricksters.

Tithes and offerings are relevant for our times now and I believe the Holy Spirit will enlighten you as you proceed on this chapter. Let's begin from where it all begun in Genesis and with the man Abraham who gave the first tithe.

Genesis 14:18-20 NLT
"And Melchizedek, the king of Salem and a priest of God Most High, brought Abram some bread and wine. Melchizedek blessed Abram with this blessing: "Blessed be Abram by God Most High, Creator of heaven and earth. And blessed be God Most High, who has defeated your enemies for you." Then Abram gave Melchizedek a tenth of all the goods he had recovered."

The background to the scripture above informs us of a war that got Abraham's nephew Lot captured and everything he owned was carried off. When Abraham heard that Lot had been captured, he mobilised his trained men and pursued after the enemy's army until he caught up with them, defeated them and recovered all the goods that had been taken away together with Lot and other captives. Abraham decided to give Melchizedek a tenth of all the goods he had recovered. The tithe (tenth) Abraham gave to Melchizedek was before God made it into a law for the children of Israel (Hebrews 7:5).

In the book of Hebrews, Jesus is like Melchizedek (Hebrews 7). Therefore if we give tithe we are giving it to Jesus (in the order of Melchizedek - Hebrews 7:11, 17) though men who will one day die receive them. And here he is referring to those who are in charge of the storehouse (church) which are the pastors. Those who were not required to pay tithe was the tribe of Levi because scripture says when Abraham gave a tithe to Melchizedek they also paid a tithe to him because they were a seed in Abraham.

Today, we who are gentiles have been engrafted in Israel because of Jesus. He came from the tribe of Judah and not Levi. Abraham considered how great Melchizedek was and gave him a tithe of what he has taken from battle. If you also recognise how great Jesus is then you must give him the tithe of all because he is in the order of Melchizedek (Hebrews 7:3). This has nothing to do with the law. If you recognise Jesus as a priest forever, then he deserves the tithe.
Jacob also made a vow or a covenant to God to give him a tenth of everything the Lord blesses him with. This was also before the law was given. "And this memorial pillar I have set up will become a place for worshiping God, and I will present to God a tenth of everything he gives me." Genesis 28:22 NLT

In the book of Leviticus, God decided to take the tithe and make it into a law for the children of Israel to obey (Leviticus 27:30-32) and so in the book of Malachi when they refused to pay the tithe and offering He said they have robbed him. And if you rob God what is due him (acknowledging him as your source of power, provider, protector, etc.) then you are definitely going to expose yourself to the attacks of the devil and when the devil attacks you the only description we can give to your life is a cursed life. That's why God said the Israelites were under a curse (Malachi 3:8-9).

Our heavenly Father does not curse anyone, that's why Jesus even said we should love our enemies (Matthew 5:44). The devil is already busy looking for someone to devour. If you don't recognise the great one who can protect and provide for you then you become an easy prey to the devil who is the destroyer of every good thing, thereby making your life a cursed life. So God said He will be in the position to rebuke the devil once you acknowledge him and give him what is due him.

Jesus in Matthew 23:23 says, "What sorrow awaits you teachers of religious law and you Pharisees. Hypocrites! For you are careful to

tithe even the tiniest income from your herb gardens, but you ignore the more important aspects of the law — justice, mercy, and faith. You should tithe, yes, but do not neglect the more important things."
Jesus affirmed tithing even when dealing with the Pharisees who were hypocrites. Don't miss out on this great opportunity.

The Covenant Side of Tithes and Offerings

My covenant will I not break, nor alter the thing that is gone out of my lips.
Psalm 89:34

God has said something regarding tithes and offerings and any word that goes out of the mouth of God which is in agreement with the New Covenant we have in Christ Jesus cannot be reversed. Look at what God says about tithes here:
"Bring ye all the tithes into the storehouse, that there may be meat in mine house, and prove me now herewith, saith the Lord of hosts, if I will not open you the windows of heaven, and pour you out a blessing, that there shall not be room enough to receive it. And I will rebuke the devourer for your sakes, and he shall not destroy the fruits of your ground; neither shall your vine cast her fruit before the time in the field, saith the Lord of hosts. And all nations shall call you blessed: for ye shall be a delightsome land, saith the Lord of hosts." Malachi 3:10-12

God has promised and since he has never lied and will never lie, it will be great to enter into a covenant with God and see the fulfillment of His promises regarding tithes and offerings in your life.

10 Reasons Why We Should Give Tithes and Offerings
1. It acknowledges God for who He is:

   The first tithe that was recorded in the Bible was by Abraham and he did it to acknowledge the greatness of the priest of God Melchizedek. "Consider then how great this Melchizedek was. Even Abraham, the great patriarch of Israel, recognised this by giving him a tenth of what he had taken in battle (Hebrews 7:4 NLT)". Today, Jesus who is God is acknowledged when we see how great He is and give Him his tithe.

2. It brings food into the Lord's storehouse:

    "Bring all the tithes into the storehouse so there will be enough food in my temple..." Malachi 3:10 NLT.

    The food in the temple is meant to cater for the work of God; for paying pastors, the strangers, the orphans and widows (Deuteronomy 14:28-29). If you refuse to give your tithe how do you expect the work of God to progress? The storehouse here also refers to your local church and not a foreign church because that is where you are fed the word of God. You go to church to be taught the word of God, when you have issues you go to the pastor to pray for you and now when you get money to pay tithe you send it elsewhere. How do you expect the pastor who feeds you to survive? Bible says, "Elders who do their work well should be respected and paid well, especially those who work hard at both preaching and teaching." (1 Timothy 5:17 NLT) Where is the money going to come from to pay them well? It therefore behoves on you to send your tithe to your local church where you fellowship.

3. It serves as a point to prove God's blessings:

    Malachi 3:10 KJV says, "Bring ye all the tithes into the storehouse, that there may be meat in mine house, and prove me now herewith, saith the Lord of hosts, if I will not open you the windows of heaven, and pour you out a blessing, that there shall not be room enough to receive it."

    God has spoken and let all the church say, Amen! Our Father is faithful and he who has promised will bring it to pass. Trust always in him and you'll see his blessings overflowing in your life.

4. It brings you protection from destruction:

Malachi 3:11 "And I will rebuke the devourer for your sakes, so that he will not destroy the fruit of your ground, nor shall the vine fail to bear fruit for you in the field," says the LORD of hosts;"

Agriculture was the main profession of the Israelites at that time and God promised to preserve their work from any devourer. Now most of us are not farmers but whatever we are involved in that brings us income the Lord will preserve it from any destruction. The devil is very busy roaming like an angry lion seeking someone to devour.

"Be sober, be vigilant; because your adversary the devil, as a roaring lion, walketh about, seeking whom he may devour: Whom resist steadfast in the faith, knowing that the same afflictions are accomplished in your brethren that are in the world." 1 Peter 5:8-9

The only way we can overcome is to resist steadfast in the faith. Giving of tithe and offering is a matter of faith and God stands by His word to rebuke the devil who is the devourer.

5. It is a seed you have planted in the Kingdom of God and it will grow:

    Tithes and offerings serve as seeds we sow in the Kingdom of God and it will germinate.

    Remember this—a farmer who plants only a few seeds will get a small crop. But the one who plants generously will get a generous crop. You must each decide in your heart how much to give. And don't give reluctantly or in response to pressure. *"For God loves a person who gives cheerfully"* 2 Corinthians 9:7 NLT. *"…You will always harvest what you plant."* Galatians 6:7 NLT. Here, our giving is equated to sowing. If you give tithes and offerings you'll surely harvest the blessings of God. The harvest can come not only in monetary form but also in diverse areas like good health, protection, favour, etc.

This is not a gamble to expect your increase right after you give your tithe and offering. Yours is to do your part according to grace and the Lord will bring the increase in his own time.

Your tithe and offering are the first point of call of being a kingdom investor. If you are able to give God your tithe then I believe whatever the Lord asks of you, you'll be able to give as well.

6. It proves our faithfulness to the Lord:

    "If you are faithful in little things, you will be faithful in large ones. But if you are dishonest in little things, you won't be honest with greater responsibilities. And if you are untrustworthy about worldly wealth, who will trust you with the true riches of heaven?" Luke 16:10, 11 NLT

    "And you shall remember the LORD your God, for it is He who gives you power to get wealth, that He may establish His covenant which He swore to your fathers, as it is this day. Deuteronomy 8:18

    Remembering the Lord for the strength and grace to make money or wealth shows how faithful we are to him and he who is faithful in little is also faithful in much. Don't wait and say if I get a big pay then I'll start paying tithe, start now with the little and prove God's faithfulness in blessing you whiles you also prove your faithfulness to handle big things with the small you give.

7. It reveals our heart:

    I heard a story of a man who loved to garden. He loved the garden so much that he would fertilise it, water it and invest in it. In one year as he was doing this, he grew the biggest carrot he had ever grown and he was proud of it. He decided to take the carrot and present it to the king. So he took it to the palace and he said to the king, "this is the greatest carrot I have ever grown, it is the best one and I want you to have it". The king discerning the man's heart understood that he was truly giving the carrot to him because he was excited about what has happened. The king looked at the man and said, 'I've understood that you are giving this not for any other reason but you want to bless me as king'. The king looked at the man and said, "I own the field next to your garden, am going to give you that field. You love the garden and I think you can do great things and am going to give it to you because of what you did."

There was a noble man in the court that day and he looked at what has happened and he thought, "Well, if this guy gave the king a carrot and look at what has happened; what if I give the king something really cool?" And this noble man raised horses. He went and got a black stallion from his herd and it was the best horse he had raised. He brought it to the king and said, "This is the best horse I've ever bred. This is the best horse I'll ever breed and there won't be another one like it. It is the greatest horse I've ever seen and I want to present it to you". The king took the horse, said thank you and walked away. He put the horse in his stable and said nothing else. The king discerned the man's heart and it wasn't about giving but he wanted to receive.

Let me teach you something, the first man came giving not to receive but simply to give. This means that God wants your heart!

God does not need your money. He's not broke but simply wants to bless you. God is looking out for the one who'll give to him cheerfully (2 Corinthians 9:6-7). Let's reveal a heart of gratitude and cheerfulness to God and we'll always see his goodness in our lives.

8. It is acceptable to God:

"As you know, you Philippians were the only ones who gave me financial help when I first brought you the Good News and then travelled on from Macedonia. No other church did this. I don't say this because I want a gift from you. Rather, I want you to receive a reward for your kindness. At the moment I have all I need—and more! I am generously supplied with the gifts you sent me with Epaphroditus. They are a sweet-smelling sacrifice that is acceptable and pleasing to God. And this same God who takes care of me will supply all your needs from his glorious riches, which have been given to us in Christ Jesus." Philippians 4:15, 17-19 NLT

Your giving serves as a sweet-smelling sacrifice that is acceptable to God. When everyone chooses not to give, be the one to give and the same God who takes care of the church will supply all your needs from his glorious riches, which has been given to us in Christ Jesus.

9. It's a form of worship:

    "Honour the Lord with your wealth and with the best part of everything you produce. Then he will fill your barns with grain, and your vats will overflow with good wine." Proverbs 3:9, 10

    In his book 'How to Enter the Throne Room of God Through Worship', Rev. Dr. Kwasi Boateng defined worship as the act of showing reverence and honour to God in spirit and truth accompanied by appropriate physical action such as bowing, kneeling, prostrating or lifting up of hands. I will also add one more physical action which is giving of substance to the Lord. The wise men came and worshiped and gave gifts to Jesus. Our gifts, offerings and tithes bring honour to God. As we go to church to worship God, let's not forget our substance as well.

    If you love God, don't expect that relationship not to cost you anything. Love gives (John 3:16) and God is also pleased to receive from you because he first loved you and gave to you first.

CHAPTER 5
GRACE FOR FORGIVENESS

We hurt and grieve the Lord every day
But He loves and forgives us any way
And does not for one, throw on us guilt and blame,
Then we know unto others, we must then do same

"For everyone has sinned; we all fall short of God's glorious standard" Romans 3:23.

Sin (missing the mark) is a nature and when you receive Christ into your heart he replaces that nature with a new nature called righteousness. Righteousness is having a right standing with God and it has nothing to do with you or what you have done but simply because Jesus Christ has made you righteous (2 Corinthians 5:21).

Imagine a child who was born and raised in a slum for about 15 years and then sent to inhabit in a well-developed community. It is obvious that considering the influence of his early years, he will behave as he used to. Example, acts like urinating anywhere, throwing rubbish around or spitting anywhere. But with time he'll conform to the lifestyle of the well-developed community. If he continues to do things with the mentality from the slum, it does not mean he is not living in a well-developed community. It is only his mindset that must change.

It is the same way with the new believer. At times you are likely to find yourself doing some of the sinful things you used to do but that does not mean you are not a citizen of heaven. For the Holy Spirit bears witness with our spirit that we are children of God (Romans 8:16). It is just a matter of acquainting yourself with the new constitution of your country which is the Bible and allowing the Holy Spirit to renew your mind (Romans 12:2).

In the scenario above, the young man's position has changed and he'll have to live happily as a citizen of the well-developed community. That is how Christ has made us, he has translated us from the kingdom of darkness into his own kingdom (Colossians 1:13). You have been translated from the nature of sin to the nature of righteousness and you need to allow God to renew your mind with what conforms to your new citizenship.

Christians who have not renewed their minds mentally are always fond of rededicating their lives to Jesus over and over again or accepting Jesus as their Lord and personal saviour every time an altar call is made. This is because of the understanding they lack about their new position in Christ. Satan also uses that opportunity to always condemn them of their wrong action thereby making them feel unworthy to come to God or receive anything from him. That's why they give their lives to Jesus over and over again. The good news says, *"So now there is no condemnation for those who belong to Christ Jesus" (Romans 8:1)*. When you know God has made you righteous in Christ Jesus no devil can deceive you from receiving everything our good Father has for us.

What you need to know is that sin is a nature and with Jesus in your heart (spirit) he has replaced that nature with his righteous spirit. Scripture says in *1 John 3:9 that, "Whosoever is born of God doth not commit sin; for his seed remaineth in him: and he cannot sin because he is born of God."* That is the truth. The nature of sin is taken away so you cannot sin. You may do something and call it "sin" but even as you approach God's throne boldly and fellowship with each other, the blood of Jesus cleanses you from all sin (Hebrews 11:24, 1 John 1:7). In this new chapter of man's relationship with God, we do not need the law to teach us what sin is but rather the Holy Spirit to lead us into all truth (John 16:13). God has forgiven our past, present and future sins. Imagine, a parent bathe a child, put nice clothes on him and allowed the child to walk around freely or even go out to have some fun. It is likely the child will return home with dirty clothes. Every good parent will take off those dirty clothes, bath the child again, put a new cloth on the child and allow the child to move freely once again. That is the way our heavenly Father deals with us. Anytime we come to him scripture says, "As we walk in the light as he is in the light we have fellowship with one another and the blood of Jesus cleanses us from all sin" (1 John 1:7). Even before you open your mouth to confess those sins, he has forgiven you. Do you remember the prodigal son in Luke 15? He realised he sinned against his father and rehearsed his repentant speech. But when the father met him, he lavished his love on him and repositioned him in the family. That is what happens when we come to the Father in prayer, study his word or church. He always cleanses us.

As we walk about in this life, by nature, we are likely to become dirty like that little child but we have been made righteous. As you begin to walk in this consciousness of righteousness, the more you live a life of ethical righteousness and that brings glory to God. As a man thinks in his heart so is he (Proverbs 23:7). The Holy Spirit has showed us who we are in the scriptures and having those thoughts of who we are is what will reflect on the outside for all to see.

A more excellent way is for every believer to know their true position in Christ Jesus. "For God made Christ, who never sinned, to be the offering for our sin, so that we could be made right with God through Christ" (2 Corinthians 5:21). By grace through Christ Jesus we have a right standing with God. Isaiah said our righteousness are as filthy rags before God (Isaiah 64:6). There is nothing about us that can please God but by his own grace through Jesus we can now stand confidently before God and have fellowship with Him. What a privilege!

Well then, should we keep on sinning so that God can show us more and more of his wonderful grace? Of course not! Since we have died to sin, how can we continue to live in it? Or have you forgotten that when we were joined with Christ Jesus in baptism, we joined him in his death? For we died and were buried with Christ by baptism. And just as Christ was raised from the dead by the glorious power of the Father, now we also may live new lives. Since we have been united with him in his death, we will also be raised to life as he was. We know that our old sinful selves were crucified with Christ so that sin might lose its power in our lives. We are no longer slaves to sin. For when we died with Christ we were set free from the power of sin. And since we died with Christ, we know we will also live with him. We are sure of this because Christ was raised from the dead, and he will never die again. Death no longer has any power over him. When he died, he died once to break the power of sin. But now that he lives, he lives for the glory of God. So you also should consider yourselves to be dead to the power of sin and alive to God through Christ Jesus. (Romans 6:1-11 NLT)

Scripture admonishes us to consider ourselves dead to sin and alive in Christ. What does it mean to consider yourself dead to sin? Paul said in Galatians 2:20, "My old self has been crucified with Christ. It is no longer I who live, but Christ lives in me. So I live in this earthly body by trusting in the Son of God, who loved me and gave himself for me." To consider yourself dead to sin is therefore to focus on Jesus Christ who now lives in you to express His life through you in all you do. **The moment you focus attention on yourself to overcome any challenge or addiction, you are not considering yourself dead and you will continue to live in that sin.**

Sin leads to death and many have been subject to bondage to the fear of death. In the Old Covenant, "the soul that sin shall die" (Ezekiel 18:20) and so the children of Israel were always careful to do the right things lest they encounter the wrath of God and die. God gave them about 600 laws to obey in order to be righteous and receive His blessings but God also knew the children of Israel could not follow through perfectly in all the laws because, "For whosoever shall keep the whole law, and yet offend in one point, he is guilty of all" (James 2:10).

Therefore, in order to bless them he required a sacrifice from them anytime they realised they missed the mark or any of the laws. By so doing God transferred their iniquity of sin unto the sacrifice which was without any blemish or fault and covered their sin so they could receive His blessings. This process went on year after year as a shadow of the perfect sacrifice which was to come. That perfect sacrifice was Jesus Christ, the Lamb of God, who was crucified once and for all time to remove our past, present and future sins forever. *"For God's will was for us to be made holy by the sacrifice of the body of Jesus Christ, once for all time. For by that one offering he forever made perfect those who are being made holy." Hebrews 10:10, 14*

Now, all that the believer has to do is to believe right and know that he is righteous before God anytime, any day and anywhere. This righteousness I am talking about is having a right standing with God and it is by faith, not something we do to earn and that is grace!

The new covenant God has with us now is not based on what we do to receive his blessings like the old covenant, for he himself has said, *"...And I will forgive their wickedness, and I will never again remember their sins" Hebrews 8:12.* David saw into this new covenant when he said, *"Oh, what joy for those whose disobedience is forgiven, whose sin is put out of sight! Yes, what joy for those whose record the Lord has cleared of guilt, whose lives are lived in complete honesty!" Psalm 32:1-2.*

When your sins are put out of sight then you are righteous and once you are righteous then you qualify for God's blessings. "For God made Christ, who never sinned, to be the offering for our sin, so that we could be made right with God through Christ." (2 Corinthians 5:21) Let this mindset be in you that you are always righteous before God and that qualifies you for all of God's blessings.

In many grace books it is common to find some discussion on 1 John 1:9. This verse is special because it is the only verse in the new covenant that appears to link confession of sins with God's forgiveness. If this verse was in the old covenant it would be no great thing, but because it's in the new it stands out.

CONFESSION OF SINS

But if we confess our sins to him, he is faithful and just to forgive us our sins and to cleanse us from all wickedness. 1 John 1:9 NLT.

This scripture is the only verse in the New Testament that talks about confession of sins. Confession is to come into agreement with God. Therefore, confession of sins is to agree with God that whatever He calls sin is sin. Our acknowledgement of that truth alone guarantees us of God's forgiveness.

There are those who teach that confession of sins is to open your mouth and tell God of all the sins you have committed for him to forgive you. What about those sins you forget to confess? Do you also know whatsoever is not of faith is sin (Romans 14:23) and he who knows what is good and does not do them is also sin (James 4:17)? Do you open your mouth and confess these sins as well? Also, how many sins did you confess before giving your life to Jesus? If your understanding is to open your mouth and say all your faults before God forgives you then you are not living a life of faith nor are you pleasing God for all that Jesus has done for you.

Jesus died for your sins before you were born and His forgiveness is forever. Whenever you know you have done something wicked, the best thing is to acknowledge you're wrong and thank God for his forgiveness and receive it because it is there for you. He said "before they call, I will answer; and whiles they are speaking, I will hear" Isaiah 65:24. Do you remember the prodigal son? He rehearsed his repentant speech but had no opportunity to say them. God loves you so much and he will in no wise cast you out if you come to him.

Some also think there is no forgiveness for them because of the wickedness they have committed. Always know that even where sin abounds, grace abounds much more (Romans 5:20). The grace of God is available to forgive you no matter your sins. Approach his throne today and obtain His mercy and grace in any area of need (Hebrews 4:12). In the new covenant He said, "For I will be merciful to their unrighteousness, and their sins and their iniquities will I remember no more" (Hebrews 8:12). This is the LORD speaking, he holds nothing against you. Embrace his love for you today and receive his forgiveness.

It is interesting to know that those who are of the mindset of verbally confessing their sins are always looking out for their sins to say them to God. The enemy takes this opportunity to point out their weaknesses and faults to them, making them live a life of condemnation, guilt, and weakness. But thanks be to God that there is no more condemnation for those who are in Christ Jesus (Romans 8:1).

God's forgiveness is there for us. If God has made you born again, who can make you unborn again? Paul said nothing can separate us from the love of God. "What shall we say about such wonderful things as these? If God is for us, who can ever be against us? Since he did not spare even his own Son but gave him up for us all, won't he also give us everything else? Who dares accuse us whom God has chosen for his own? No one – for God himself has given us right standing with himself. Who then will condemn us? No one – for Christ Jesus died for us and was raised to life for us, and he is sitting in the place of honour at God's right hand, pleading for us.

Can anything ever separate us from Christ's love? Does it mean he no longer loves us if we have trouble or calamity, or are persecuted, or hungry, or destitute, or in danger, or threatened with death? (As the Scriptures say, "For your sake we are killed every day; we are being slaughtered like sheep.") No, despite all these things, overwhelming victory is ours through Christ, who loved us.

And I am convinced that nothing can ever separate us from God's love. Neither death nor life, neither angels nor demons, neither our fears for today nor our worries about tomorrow – not even the powers of hell can separate us from God's love. No power in the sky above or in the earth below – indeed, nothing in all creation will ever be able to separate us from the love of God that is revealed in Christ Jesus our Lord" Romans 8:31-39.
Your actions cannot separate you from the love of God. You are born again, you are a saint, you are sanctified, you are righteous, you are holy and you are in the Kingdom of God because of Jesus. Receive His love today and enjoy His grace for forgiveness.

CHAPTER 6
GRACE FOR MARRIAGE

"To respect, to love, to cherish and to hold"
These words have existed since the days of old
The ability to perform all duties needed to be done
Is made possible since God intended the two to be one

"The man who finds a wife finds a treasure and he receives favour from the LORD" Proverbs 18:22 NLT.

God makes grace available for every godly marriage. I will be sharing with you ten significant areas through which God's grace is expressed in every godly marriage.

1.   Grace for Loving her

"For husbands, this means love your wives, just as Christ loved the church. He gave up his life for her to make her holy and clean, washed by the cleansing of God's word." (Ephesians 5:25, 26 NLT)
You loved her before you married her and so why should the Holy Spirit record that you must love your wife? This clearly shows that love is likely to diminish or decline in marriage but God has made it clear that husbands should continue to love their wives and I believe God makes grace available to love her more. Rely on Christ-in-you to express his love through you to love her.
No matter the sins we committed Christ Jesus gave up His life for the church in order to make her holy and clean, washed by the cleansing of God's word. Husbands, there is grace available for sacrificial love. You must love your wife unconditionally. The command to love is not

contingent upon how your wife is living out the part of her covenant. It is a matter of obedience, disobedience is not an option. No matter the wrong she has done to you, forgive her and cleanse her through God's word and you'll see the goodness of the Lord in your marriage.

2.   Grace for Respecting him

...and the wife must respect her husband. Ephesians 5:33
If it was not possible for a wife to show respect to the husband, I believe God will not make mention of it. The greatest need of every man is respect and many marriages are ruined because of this attribute which is missing in many wives of today.
The respect you give your husband is not based on whether he loves you or not but it should be in response to God's word and the vows you made before God. Your husband needs not earn your respect before you give it. Unconditional respect means just that. This does not mean you are a fool to an unbearable, undeserving husband but rather it is to show your faith and trust in God's word to lead you through your marriage. Allow "Christ-in-you" to live the life of respect through you. No matter the challenges, treat him good, respect him and you'll surely have your marriage soaring higher.

3.   Grace for Leadership

Married couples are to demonstrate leadership in their marriages and more importantly the man must take the lead. In the Garden of Eden, God told the man everything he had to do before Eve came on the scene. Therefore, it was the responsibility of Adam to teach Eve what was required of her as a wife.
Every husband must take the lead to receive from God and be able to teach the wife. You must be the "eye" or visionary and leader of the family. When husbands take their rightful places of leadership the family is blessed, society is blessed and the nation is blessed.

The greatest challenge on the continent of Africa is leadership and the root cause is simply because most men are not being responsible to take the lead in their homes. Many fathers in Africa have no dignity because they have neglected their wives and children and have not taken up the responsibility of leading the family but I see the story of Africa being retold in Jesus name. When the family spends quality time with the Lord, he leads and directs them on the right path and all is by His grace. The Lord says *"I will guide you along the best pathway for your life. I will advise you and watch over you"* (Psalm 32:8).

4.   Grace for Sanctification

....to make her holy and clean, washed by the cleansing of God's word. Ephesians 5:26
The grace of God is available to cleanse and sanctify every marriage. The word of God is like water that cleanses us from all impurities. Jesus admonished the husbands to cleanse their wives therefore it behoves every husband to know the word of God. Thereby cleansing themselves first and then sharing it with their wives to cleanse them as well. We cannot become clean by our own efforts but spiritually God's grace cleanses us as we read and study his word. Couples must make it a point to make the word of God a part of their everyday lives.

5.   Grace for Leaving and Cleaving

The whole duty of marriage as expressed by marriage counsellor Eugene Addison is in Genesis 2:24. *"Therefore shall a man leave his father and his mother, and shall cleave unto his wife: and they shall be one flesh." Genesis 2:24*
God makes grace available for a man to leave his family, friends, and other associations to be united to his wife. To cleave means to cling or adhere, to fasten together, to follow close after, or to stick. God by His grace makes the couple one as the man cleaves to his wife. God makes you one in body and spirit as you depend on him. It's very nice when you see some couples and they look alike. It's as if they are from one parent and truly they have one Father the Lord almighty. Depend on him for oneness or unity in purpose, love, selflessness, romance, understanding, etc. and his grace makes all that available.

6.   Grace for Fruitfulness and Multiplication

"Then God blessed them and said, "Be fruitful and multiply. Fill the earth and govern it. Reign over the fish in the sea, the birds in the sky, and all the animals that scurry along the ground."" Genesis 1:28 NLT

"Now be fruitful and multiply, and repopulate the earth."
Genesis 9:7
"Children are a gift from the Lord; they are a reward from him." Psalm 127:3

Our Father by His goodness has filled us with the ability to be fruitful and multiply. Marriage is God's design to bring about fruitfulness between a man and a woman. The principle for fruitfulness and multiplication cannot be limited to reproduction of babies only. It also symbolises progress, enlargement, growth, development, increase, ingenuity, abundance, prosperity and technology.

What God therefore is implying is that not only will you give birth but the grace to feed those children is also available. This grace is manifested in the work we do, the ideas to bring about technology to enhance destiny, and also the beauty of synergy *"two are better than one because they have a good reward for their labour" (Ecclesiastes 4:9).*
Psalm 128:3 says, *"Your wife will be like a fruitful grapevine, flourishing within your home. Your children will be like vigorous young olive trees as they sit around your table."* Embrace this scripture and declare it into your life and marriage. Declaration is one of the ways to see the word of God come to pass in your life and it all happens by his grace.

7. Grace for Submission

"And further, submit to one another out of reverence for Christ. For wives, this means submit to your husbands as to the Lord. For a husband is the head of his wife as Christ is the head of the church. He is the Saviour of his body, the church. As the church submits to Christ, so you wives should submit to your husbands in everything. Ephesians 5:21-24 NLT
Merriam-Webster dictionary defines submission as yielding oneself to the authority or will of another. In life, everyone submits to something. It can be your government, teacher, husband, wife, doctor, manager, driver, mother, father, pastor, customer, etc. Scripture makes us understand we need to submit one to another (Ephesians 5:21) and for wives this is expressed in submitting to their husbands and to the husbands it means to love their wives.

It becomes easy and lovely to yield to the authority of another when we rely on the grace of God to do so. Every wife should believe and declare, "By the grace of God I am submissive to my husband yet not I but Christ in me" and husbands should also believe and declare "By the grace of God I love my wife yet not I but Christ in me". Relying on the grace of God is the best way to live a fulfilled life and to enjoy a happy marriage.

8. Grace for Romance, Love and Affection

Someone is thinking, does God care so much about romance? Yes, He does.

"Let your wife be a fountain of blessing for you. Rejoice in the wife of your youth. She is a loving deer, a graceful doe. Let her breasts satisfy you always. May you always be captivated by her love". Proverbs 5:18-19

"Now Adam had sexual relations with his wife, Eve, and she became pregnant...." Genesis 4:1

"You are beautiful, my darling, beautiful beyond words. Your eyes are like doves behind your veil. Your hair falls in waves, like a flock of goats winding down the slopes of Gilead." Song of Songs 4:1 NLT

God gave our first parents the gift of sex and blessed them. Don't let anyone deceive you on this matter. The grace of God enables us to be more romantic, loving and affectionate in our marriage. Scripture says, *"While we were yet sinners Christ died for us" (Romans 5:8)*. Your partner needs not be perfect before you engage in romantic acts. Even if he or she has offended you rely on God's grace to forgive because it is Christ in you (Galatians 2:20) that does the work of forgiveness through you to love and to be romantic despite the offense. If we rely on this grace of God I believe there will be no divorce. Roderick C. Meredith said, "We all need to view marriage as a kind of "workshop" to teach us how to give, how to share and how to forgive others on a continual basis" and I add that all can be done by appropriating the grace of our Lord Jesus Christ.

9. Grace for Communication

.... Let me see your face; let me hear your voice. For your voice is pleasant, and your face is lovely. Song of Songs 2:14 NLT

It is said that communication is the life blood of every relationship. It is good to greet each other every morning when you wake up, wish the best for each other throughout the day, welcome each other when you meet in the evening after work and talk about what transpired at work. You will be able to communicate effectively, efficiently and positively when you rely on the grace of God.

You need to be willing to take time to really "listen" to your mate-showing genuine interest in what your sweetheart is saying or going through. Loving positive flow of communication, information and sharing of plans and dreams between a husband and wife is the very essence of a happy marriage and the grace of God makes it happen excellently.

10. Grace for Commitment and Trust

"Since they are no longer two but one, let no one split apart what God has joined together." Matthew 19:6 NLT

"You cry out, "Why doesn't the Lord accept my worship?" I'll tell you why! Because the Lord witnessed the vows you and your wife made when you were young. But you have been unfaithful to her, though she remained your faithful partner, the wife of your marriage vows." Malachi 2:14 NLT

Marriage is a lifelong decision and it is only the grace of God that unites both of you forever. You will also have to be committed to your various responsibilities as couples and above all trust each other to fulfill destiny together.

My good friend Mr. C.O.C Otu-Amate, an author and a retired diplomat, with his wife celebrated their 57th marriage anniversary the year 2014. Mr. Otu-Amate   92 years old as of the year 2015 did not look like a 92 year old man. One thing I admire about him is the friendship and love between him and his wife. Any time I visit their home grandpa and grandma are always together and all I see is the grace of God at work in their lives. Their eyes are not dim nor their natural strength abated. Grandpa likes reading the Bible, writing and does a lot on social media (Facebook, LinkedIn and Twitter) to promote the sales of his books.

Beloved, keep up the commitment, maintenance and trust in your marriage and you'll surely succeed, yet not you at work but the grace of God at work in you.

CHAPTER 7
GRACE FOR RESTORATION

All the good things we lost and sadly passed us by
The wonderful things we missed that made us cry
The great things and even the ones seemingly small
There is surely a power that makes us recover all

God never changes; he is the same yesterday, today and forever. He is still in the business of restoring anything that has been lost. John 10:10 says, *"The thief's purpose is to steal and kill and destroy. My purpose is to give them a rich and satisfying life."* Jesus has that rich and satisfying life with him.

The good news is if you are in Christ Jesus, you have been restored! Hallelujah!! However, many people who are in Christ Jesus (Christians) find it difficult to understand this new position of being restored. They look at their present circumstances and complain that all is not well. They might be facing challenges in their health, relationship, finance, education, etc. and think nothing has changed after giving their lives to Jesus.

Beloved, the purpose of Jesus in your life is to restore you to that dignifying place or position of glory (Romans 3:23) mankind lost through sin. If Jesus is in you be assured you are restored in whatever area you are lacking or whatever was stolen from you by the devil because on the cross he said it is finished. He completed His work of redemption on the cross of Calvary. Your sickness, shame, poverty, lack, worry, curse or any negative thing from the devil was destroyed on the cross.

That is why Jesus said it is finished!

59

But Kojo, why do I get sick and broke at times even though Jesus has finished his work of redemption in my life?

Very good question. As long as we are in this body, we are bound to face challenges of fatigue, pain, stress, etc. but that is not conclusive. That is why it is important for everyone to be saved. With Jesus in your life you have the legal right to believe and declare what he has done for you regarding that issue. For instance, 1 Peter 2:24 tells us that by His stripes we are healed. Hold on to His Word and declare it against that sickness. Believe in the word of God to heal and set you free and you'll be made whole.

On finance, Jesus became poor that you might become rich (2 Corinthians 8:9). Believe what the word of God says about you and declare your stand. More of this is in the chapter on the 'Finished Works of Jesus'. Also, regarding issues on money, note that when you sow you reap (2 Corinthians 9:6). Don't faint in your giving (Galatians 6:9) and you'll surely reap bountifully.

There are quite a number of dynamics when it comes to money matters. You need to understand tithing, offering, sowing, giving, investing, budgeting and planning. You can call on a resourceful person in such areas to assist you.

In conclusion, note that it is the Lord who gives you power to get wealth (Deuteronomy 8:18) and such power is an act of his grace. As I said earlier, Jesus has restored you. If you find shortfalls in some areas of your life, search the scriptures and know what Jesus has done about that and declare it over that situation. The Lord who has exalted his word above his name (Psalm 138:2) will ensure it comes to pass in your life. Amen!

CHAPTER 8
GRACE FOR LEADERSHIP

That guide that shows you the right way
And the filling of words for what to say
If to every word of God we should heed,
We will realise there is grace to be led so we lead

Lead on Jesus....I will follow you!

Jesus Christ is the true light who gives light to everyone that comes into the world (John 1:9). No matter your field of endeavour, when you follow the light (Jesus), you'll come out successfully.

Leadership begins with you. Until you lead yourself successfully in the light that Jesus provides, no one will be willing to follow your lead. Leadership for the past many years has been the greatest challenge on the continent of Africa. By this book I want to assure you there is grace available for excellent leadership.

There are certain key qualities that are common to every successful leader and the grace of God expresses itself in all these areas. I'll be sharing with you 10 key qualities of a great leader and how God makes his grace available in all these areas.

1. Grace for Service:

    Leadership is service and service is work. Service is one quality that distinguishes one for excellent leadership. Every leader who serves faithfully today leaves a legacy for tomorrow. Jesus the great master and leader came not to be served but to serve. God makes his grace available for service. Look at what Paul said in I Corinthians 15:10, *"But by the grace of God I am what I am, and His grace towards me was not in vain; but I laboured more abundantly than they all, yet not I, but the grace of God which was with me."* Receive God's grace for excellent service today.

2. Grace for Vision:

Every great leader has a vision. Vision here is the ability to see or think about or plan the future with imagination or wisdom. The Lord by his grace can cause you to see the future in your life, family, organisation or any project for you to plan appropriately. Not all leaders are able to see the future but the grace of God can cause you to see. Jeremiah 33:3 says, *"Call to me, and I will answer you, and show you great and mighty things, which you do not know."* The favour Jeremiah found with God enabled him to have access into the future. You are favoured because of Jesus Christ. Ask the Father and He'll be glad to show you the future.

3. Grace for Protection:

Protection is very crucial for leadership. Be aware that it's not everyone who is happy where you are but when God's grace locates you, His favour becomes like a shield all around you (Psalm 5:12) and the devil cannot do you any harm. Understand your position in Christ as I've shared in the next chapter 'Grace for warfare' and be rest assured that your position is secured by the blood of Jesus.

4. Grace for Discernment:

Every leader meets and works with different people. It will only take the grace of God to know the right people to engage in business or even share ideas with. The Holy Spirit is with us to guide us into all truth (John 16:13). Rely on him for discernment.

5. Grace for Decision Making & Guidance:

What makes an excellent leader is the ability to make wise decisions. The LORD says, *"I will guide you along the best pathway for your life. I will advise you and watch over you." (Psalm 32:8 NLT)*. Rely on His guidance for your life, family, business and all other decisions you will ever make. He, the LORD, teaches you what is best for you (Isaiah 48:17) and he does that by his grace.

6. Grace for Commitment to Excellence:

Your ability to stay at the cutting edge causes you to soar higher and higher in leadership. Great businesses and organisations have shown commitment to excellence and today they cannot be taken for granted. The LORD showed Joshua how to stay at the cutting edge by telling him not to let the book of the law depart from his mouth and also to be sure to do all that is written in it (Joshua 1:8). God also told Cain that, if you do well, will you not be accepted? (Genesis 4:7). Declare the right words; rely on His grace to do well in all your endeavours and excellence will be your portion.

7. Grace for Wisdom:

"Wisdom is the principal thing; therefore get wisdom: and in all your getting, get understanding". (Proverbs 4:7). It takes the wise to lead. In case you lack wisdom in any area of your leadership, God is willing to make it available for you (James 1:5). God has made Jesus to be our wisdom (1 Corinthians 1:30) and we have the mind of Christ (1 Corinthians 2:16). The wisdom that comes from Jesus is above all categories of wisdom. Wisdom enhances creativity (Exodus 28:3, 31:3-4,6; 35:26; 36:1), it builds your life, family or business (Proverbs 24:3), it brings peace (1 Kings 5:12), deliverance (Ecclesiastes 9:15), wealth and long life (Proverbs 3:16) and many more. Utilise the wisdom of Jesus in you and become a better leader.

8. Grace for Integrity:

   The Merriam-Webster Dictionary defines integrity as the quality of being honest and fair. Integrity is having strong moral principles and moral uprightness. Lack of integrity leads to distrust in leaders. In John 1:17 scripture says, *"For the law was given through Moses; grace and truth came through Jesus Christ."* Truth is always on the side of grace and Jesus supplies both of them. Receive His grace and truth today to lead with integrity.

9. Grace for Exemplary Character:

   It is said that people don't care how much you know until they know how much you care. Every great leader demonstrates a character worth emulating. Depend on Jesus to demonstrate his character through you (Galatians 5:22) to be loving, joyful, peaceful, kind, patient, good, faithful, gentle and self-controlled.

10. Grace for Courage & Confidence:

   Every great leader exhibits courage and confidence. Scripture says the righteous are bold as a lion (Proverbs 28:1).

   Jesus makes you righteous (2 Corinthians 5:21) therefore you have no excuse to be timid. Don't be afraid of their faces (Jeremiah 1:8). You must make bold decisions and strive to make your leadership one of excellence.

   Final word: The mark of every great leader is to leave the next generation better than what he came to meet. It will only take the grace of God to leave a mark of excellence and a landmark for the next generation after you to follow.

CHAPTER 9
GRACE FOR WARFARE

The enemy's deceitful plans and schemes
And of every evil that seeks to destroy
To kill, to devour and to harm
But there is enough grace to overcome

"Then I heard a loud voice shouting across the heavens, "It has come at last —
salvation and power and the Kingdom of our God, and the authority of his
Christ. For the accuser of our brothers and sisters has been thrown down to
earth — the one who accuses them before our God day and night. And they
*have defeated him by the **blood of the Lamb** and by **their testimony**. And*
they did not love their lives so much that they were afraid to die. Therefore,
rejoice, O heavens! And you, who live in the heavens, rejoice! But terror will
come on the earth and the sea, for the devil has come down to you in great
anger, knowing that he has little time."
Revelation 12:10-12 NLT

Beloved, whether you like it or not as long as you are on this earth you
are engaged in a battle with the devil. But the good news is that the
battle has already been won by JESUS (Colossians 2:15, Hebrews 2:14)
and so we are admonished in the scriptures to fight only one battle
and that battle is what the scriptures call "the good fight of faith" (1
Timothy 6:12).
In the scriptures we read above in Revelation, the heavens overcame
the devil by the BLOOD OF THE LAMB and by their TESTIMONY
and they encouraged those in heaven to rejoice but those on earth
should only expect terror. It is important for us to understand our true
nature and position as Christians. When you read your Bible you'll
come by some verses which say "we are in Christ" and other verses

also say "Christ is in us". For instance, in Colossians 1:27 scripture says, "To whom God would make known what is the riches of the glory of this mystery among the Gentiles; which **IS CHRIST IN YOU**, the hope of glory:" Also in Ephesians 2:6 scripture says, "And hath raised us up together, and made us sit together in heavenly places **IN CHRIST JESUS.**"

Don't be confused! It is telling us something about our position in Christ Jesus. Christ living in us is for our earthly position. He in us enables us to do and overcome challenges and situations to His glory. The great wonder and joy of grace is that when we are in Jesus, becoming joint heirs with him, we gain protection from the Father.

We-in-Christ talks about our true spiritual position which is in heaven. Therefore, if scripture encourages those in heaven to rejoice because the accuser has been cast down, we also need to rejoice because we are seated in Christ in the heavenly realms.

Here on earth, Christ is in us to help us live that life of victory he won on the cross. In heaven they overcame by the BLOOD OF THE LAMB and THEIR TESTIMONY. These two weapons they used to defeat the devil are available for us here on earth.

How do you employ these weapons to overcome the devil?

1. The BLOOD OF THE LAMB: In the Old Testament, before the children of Israel left Egypt, God said He was going to strike the Egyptians with the last plague that will ensure their exit from Egypt but they were required to kill a lamb and smear their doorpost with the blood because an angel of death will be released to kill the first born of anyone who does not have the blood on his or her doorpost (Exodus 12:12-23).

   Now, the true Lamb of God has been sacrificed and by His blood we are overcomers. The Lord was showing me something about the blood recently that I did not know before. People think the devil is wicked than God and they forget God created the devil. If God created the devil then He is wicked than the devil but he chooses to show His loving kindness to us because of Jesus. If God told the angel who was in charge of death not to kill anyone with the mark of the blood on their doorpost, how much more the devil who does not belong to his host to touch anyone with the mark of the blood of Jesus on his or her life? He has no opportunity friend!

Therefore, we overcome the devil by appropriating the blood of Jesus as a mark on our lives, household, business and anything we want the blood to preserve because when the devil sees the blood, he has no option but to pass by. The devil is defeated. He does not always play by the rules and so will come around *like* an angry lion seeking someone to devour but glory be to God that the BLOOD OF JESUS secures our victory in Christ.

2. Their TESTIMONY: The Merriam-Webster Dictionary defines testimony as a public profession of religious experience. Many people go by this definition to share an experience they came out victorious to the church or public as their testimony. But I would like you to know that it's just one aspect of testimony. Testimony is to profess or declare or confess the word of God to yourself any day, anytime and anywhere. We are surrounded by a great cloud of witnesses (Hebrews 12:1) and therefore when we confess the testimony we have about what Jesus has done for us, the spiritual world understands what we are saying. The way to overcome the devil by your testimony is to know who you are in Christ and what Jesus has done for you concerning any situation you are facing by believing and declaring it as your testimony and the devil cannot; but to flee (James 4:7).

Final word: It is important to assume a state of rest when you utilise your weapons against any activities of the devil because it is God who is fighting the good fight on your behalf. That is the only sure way you'll see your enemies defeated. This is surely Grace Warfare.

CHAPTER 10
GRACE REVEALED THROUGH COMMUNION

It moves beyond just a drink and a piece of bread
To blood and body that quickens all that's dead
The power that the communion reveals
Is one that forgives, restores and simply heals

"For I pass on to you what I received from the Lord himself. On the night when he was betrayed, the Lord Jesus took some bread and gave thanks to God for it. Then he broke it in pieces and said, "This is my body, which is given for you. Do this to remember me." In the same way, he took the cup of wine after supper, saying, "This cup is the new covenant between God and his people – an agreement confirmed with my blood. Do this to remember me as often as you drink it." For every time you eat this bread and drink this cup, you are announcing the Lord's death until he comes again.

So anyone who eats this bread or drinks this cup of the Lord unworthily is guilty of sinning against the body and blood of the Lord. That is why you should examine yourself before eating the bread and drinking the cup. For if you eat the bread or drink the cup without honouring the body of Christ, you are eating and drinking God's judgment upon yourself. That is why many of you are weak and sick and some have even died.

But if we would examine ourselves, we would not be judged by God in this way. Yet when we are judged by the Lord, we are being disciplined so that we will not be condemned along with the world.
So, my dear brothers and sisters, when you gather for the Lord's Supper, wait for each other. If you are really hungry, eat at home so you won't bring judgment upon yourselves when you meet together. I'll give you instructions about the other matters after I arrive." 1 Corinthians 11:23-34

Scripture admonishes us every time we partake of the communion to remember the Lord. The Lord Jesus accomplished a lot of things for us and they are affirmed in our lives through the communion. I have shared some few things we can remember in the body and also in the blood of Jesus so we become knowledgeable every time we partake of the Holy Communion.

Benefits through the Body of Christ
1.   Communion affirms our Eternal Life

John 6:53, 54 NLT

"So Jesus said again, "I tell you the truth, unless you eat the flesh of the Son of Man and drink his blood, you cannot have eternal life within you. But anyone who eats my flesh and drinks my blood has eternal life, and I will raise that person at the last day."

2.   Communion opens our Spiritual Insight

Luke 24:30, 31 NLT

As they sat down to eat, he took the bread and blessed it. Then he broke it and gave it to them. Suddenly, their eyes were opened, and they recognised him. And at that moment he disappeared!

3.   Communion affirms that our sins were borne in his body

1 Peter 2:24a NLT

He personally carried our sins in his body on the cross so that we can be dead to sin and live for what is right.

4.   Communion affirms our Healing

1 Peter 2:24b NLT

By his wounds you are healed.

5. Communion affirms our Holiness

    Hebrews 10:10 NLT

    For God's will was for us to be made holy by the sacrifice of the body of Jesus Christ, once for all time.

6. Communion affirms our Sanctification

    Hebrews 10:10, 14

    By the which will we are sanctified through the offering of the body of Jesus Christ once for all. For by one offering he hath perfected for ever them that are sanctified.

Benefits through the Blood of Jesus

1. Communion affirms the Life we have in Christ

    Leviticus 17:11 NLT

    For the life of the body is in its blood. I have given you the blood on the altar to purify you, making you right with the Lord. It is the blood, given in exchange for a life, that makes purification possible.

2. Communion affirms our Victory

    Revelation 12:11 NLT

    And they have defeated him by the blood of the Lamb and by their testimony. And they did not love their lives so much that they were afraid to die.

3. Communion affirms the New Covenant we have with God

    I Corinthians 11:25

    In the same manner he also took the cup after supper, saying, "This cup is the new covenant in my blood. This do, as often as you drink it, in remembrance of me.

4.   Communion affirms our Protection

Exodus 12:13 NLT

But the blood on your doorposts will serve as a sign, marking the houses where you are staying. When I see the blood, I will pass over you. This plague of death will not touch you when I strike the land of Egypt.

5.   Communion affirms our Peace in the Lord

Colossians 1:19, 20 NLT

For God in all his fullness was pleased to live in Christ, and through him God reconciled everything to himself. He made peace with everything in heaven and on earth by means of Christ's blood on the cross.

6.   Communion   affirms   our   Eternal   Redemption (Col 1:14, Rev 5:9) Ephesians 1:7 NLT

He is so rich in kindness and grace that he purchased our freedom with the blood of his Son and forgave our sins.

7.   Communion affirms that we are Justified

Romans 5:9 KJV

Much more then, being now justified by his blood, we shall be saved from wrath through him.

8.   Communion affirms the Boldness we have

Hebrews 10:19 NLT

And so, dear brothers and sisters, we can boldly enter heaven's most holy place because of the blood of Jesus.

9. Communion affirms our Access to God

Romans 5:2

By whom also we have access by faith into this grace wherein we stand, and rejoice in hope of the glory of God.

10. Communion affirms our Forgiveness of sins

Hebrews 9:22 NLT

In fact, according to the law of Moses, nearly everything was purified with blood. For without the shedding of blood, there is no forgiveness.

11. Communion affirms the Better Things we have in Christ

Hebrews 12:24 KJV

And to Jesus the mediator of the new covenant, and to the blood of sprinkling, that speaketh better things than that of Abel.

12. Communion affirms our Nearness with God

Ephesians 2:13 NLT

But now you have been united with Christ Jesus. Once you were far away from God, but now you have been brought near to him through the blood of Christ.

13. Communion affirms the Perfection we have in every good

work

Hebrews 13:20, 21 NLT

Now the God of peace, that brought again from the dead our Lord Jesus, that great shepherd of the sheep, through the blood of the everlasting covenant, Make you perfect in every good work to do his will, working in you that which is well pleasing in his sight, through Jesus Christ; to whom be glory for ever and ever. Amen.

It is important that one partakes of the Holy Communion as often as he or she can because we do it in remembrance of all the things our Lord Jesus did for us by his grace and we announce his death... "For every time you eat this bread and drink this cup, you are announcing the Lord's death until he comes again." The devil is afraid of us announcing the death of Christ, because through death he destroyed the devil who had the power of death (Hebrews 2:14). Beloved, keep announcing the victory and the grace we have in Jesus Christ by partaking of the Holy Communion.

CHAPTER 11
GRACE REVEALED THROUGH THE PRINCIPLE OF NOTHING

Being made aware not of the things we have done
Or the things we think with our strength we can
But to know that for everything that we gain
There is a grace working for us we can't seem to explain

"Christianity is what God does for us," Evans Darko-Mensah.

Many Christians don't know what the new covenant really talks about and so tend to mix the old and new covenants together, whiles God has made the old covenant obsolete, out of date and will soon disappear. (Hebrews 8:13)

Hebrews 8:10-12 talks about what the new covenant says:

"But this is the new covenant I will make with the people of Israel on that day, says the Lord: I will put my laws in their minds, and I will write them on their hearts. I will be their God, and they will be my people. And they will not need to teach their neighbours, nor will they need to teach their relatives, saying, 'You should know the Lord.' For everyone, from the least to the greatest, will know me already. And I will forgive their wickedness, and I will never again remember their sins.'"

Christianity is about what God does for us and note the number of times God uses the word "I Will" in the scripture above. In the old covenant the burden was placed on the people "to do" without God's grace and they could not do everything God told them to do. This was not a deliberate attempt by God to burden the Israelites with conditions but they called for it out of pride.

For instance, before the Sinaitic covenant, every time the children of Israel complained and murmured they encountered God's fresh favour. When God brought them out of Israel they complained and murmured against God but He did not punish them but rather opened up the Red Sea and they crossed over to the other side on a dry ground.

At Marah, the children of Israel complained and murmured again against God. Murmuring and complaining are sins but God still showed them favour by telling Moses to drop a stick into the bitter waters and the bitter waters were made sweet. All these period Israel was enjoying the Abrahamic covenant of God not based on their performance but on God's grace.
Something remarkable happened when the children of Israel out of pride decided to do whatever the Lord tells them to do. In Exodus 19:8, the people cried out to Moses saying, "All that The Lord has spoken we will do." This ushered in the Sinaitic Covenant based on what they must do to merit for God's blessings but in the beginning it was not so.

God gave the law to bring man to the end of himself so that he would see his need for a Saviour. No matter how hard we strive to be perfect by our own actions we will fail.
Jesus always demonstrated the Principle of Nothing through His life and ministry. Take a closer look at the following scriptures:

- **John 5:19**

    So Jesus explained, "I tell you the truth, the son can do nothing by himself. He does only what he sees the Father doing. Whatever the Father does, the Son also does."

- **John 5:30**

    I can do nothing on my own. I judge as God tells me. Therefore, my judgment is just, because I carry out the will of the one who sent me, not my own will.

- **John 8:28, 29**

  So Jesus said, "When you have lifted up the son of man on the cross, then you will understand that I am he. I do nothing on my own but say only what the Father taught me. And the one who sent me is with me — he has not deserted me. For I always do what pleases him."

- **John 15:5**

  "Yes, I am the vine; you are the branches. Those who remain in me, and I in them, will produce much fruit. For apart from me you can do nothing."

The Principle of Nothing acknowledges the grace and power of God to do the impossible. It is to rely on the Lord Jesus to do anything in and through you. The result Jesus will produce through you will be far better than to do it without him. Rely on His grace today and experience his goodness in your life. *"To whom God would make known what is the riches of the glory of this mystery among the Gentiles, which is Christ in you, the hope of glory" Colossians 1:27.* Allow Jesus to work in you and through you and the results you'll achieve will be far more than if you had done it by yourself.

Fruitfulness Revealed In the Principle of Nothing
"Fruitfulness is manifesting Christ," Evans Darko-Mensah.

"Then God blessed them and said, "Be fruitful and multiply..." Genesis 1:28

The idea of Fruitfulness came from God and He spoke concerning man to "be Fruitful". The only thing that prevents man from becoming fruitful is sin. However, if you are in Christ then nothing prevents you from becoming fruitful because Jesus has dealt with sin.

God's idea of being fruitful in the New Covenant

In the new covenant, the idea of fruitfulness is different from what the old covenant depicted. Fruitfulness is not getting material things or giving birth to more children. A clear example about Jesus teaching fruitfulness in seen in the gospel of John.

"I am the true vine, and my father is the vinedresser. Every branch in me that does not bear fruit he takes away; and every branch that bears fruit he prunes, that it may bear more fruit. You are already clean because of the word which I have spoken to you. Abide in me, and I in you. As the branch cannot bear fruit of itself, unless it abides in the vine, neither can you, unless you abide in Me. "I am the vine, you are the branches. He who abides in me, and I in him, bears much fruit; for without me you can do nothing. If anyone does not abide in me, he is cast out as a branch and is withered; and they gather them and throw them into the fire, and they are burned. If you abide in me, and my words abide in you, you will ask what you desire, and it shall be done for you. By this my father is glorified, that you bear much fruit; so you will be my disciples." John 15:1-8 NKJV

Jesus outlined the conditions of fruitfulness in the above scriptures. Fruitfulness means to bear (carry). To bear or carry fruit is different from to produce fruit. The Greek word to bear is *pherō* which means to carry. Jesus expects us to carry the fruit he produces as branches.

The branches only hold and display the fruit. It does not produce the fruit. Jesus said he is the vine. Every tree has three main parts; root, stem and leaves. These three parts produce the fruit and the branches only carry the fruit. It is Jesus who produces the fruit of righteousness, compassion, love, joy, peace, goodness, etc. in our lives and we only carry the fruit to show the world of what Jesus has produced in us. Fruitfulness is to show Jesus in your life.

The Holy Spirit, who is also the Spirit of Christ in us, is the one who produces the fruit or Christ-like character. The Father who is the vinedresser will come and inspect the branch (your life) from time to time to see whether it produces fruit (Jesus' character). If the fruit shows Jesus, he prunes it for it to produce more fruit. The pruning is a form of taking any challenging habits or ungodly characters in your life. When you humble yourself for Jesus to live his life through you, aspects in your life that does not show Jesus is cut off or pruned by God. The more you focus on Jesus, the more you allow yourself to be pruned for you to bear Christ-like fruits.

Is materialism fruitfulness?

No! Materialism is not fruitfulness. A lot of Christians think when they get a lot of material things then they are being fruitful. That is wrong. Getting material things does not mean you are approved of God. It is man, who looks at the outward appearance, He, the Lord looks at the heart (inner man). The motive of getting material things needs to change. Ask yourself, why do you need more cars, more lands and more money? If the purpose is to prove a point to someone or for selfish purposes then you have missed it.

Prosperity is already there for Christians. Everything Jesus has is ours. We are joint heirs with Christ (Romans 8:17). It's not now that we are going to get them. God is willing to manifest his abundance of material blessings in our lives if we have a good motive for them. Taking your portion of the wealth to promote His kingdom and to improve the lives of people is a good opportunity for Him to grant your request. The day Ruth married Boaz her economic and social status changed. She changed from a poor woman to become the richest woman. *"For this reason a man shall leave his father and mother and be joined to his wife, and the two shall become one flesh. This is a great mystery: but I speak* **concerning Christ and the church.**" *Ephesians 5:31, 32 NKJV*

We are the church and we are united to Jesus who owns all the material things in this world. Therefore, all the material things belong to us. We don't have to beg God for them nor envy one another. Just produce Jesus' fruit in your life and all these things will be added to you (Mathew 6:33). Don't allow the devil to deceive you with material things. They all belong to Jesus and they are yours. Only have the right motive for them and the Father will express them in your life. And this is all by His grace.

CHAPTER 12
GRACE REVEALED THROUGH THE FINISHED WORKS OF JESUS

The most important of all is to know Jesus
And the exceeding power of His name
One that cleanses, purifies, heals
And takes away every guilt and shame

"Jesus knew that his mission was now finished, and to fulfill scripture he said, "I am thirsty." A jar of sour wine was sitting there, so they soaked a sponge in it, put it on a hyssop branch, and held it up to his lips. When Jesus had tasted it, he said, "It is finished!" Then he bowed his head and released his spirit." John 19:28-30 NLT

Before Jesus died on the cross he said, "IT IS FINISHED". This means all your problems and challenges are over because he took all of them away. When Jesus was on earth he spent 33 years and for this reason I have outlined 33 things Jesus did for us before he ascended to the Father though they are more than 33. Meditate on these finished works of Jesus Christ and your life will never be the same again.

1. Jesus became sin that I might become the righteousness of God.

   2 Corinthians 5:21
   For he hath made him to be sin for us, who knew no sin; that we might be made the righteousness of God in him.

2. Jesus has brought me divine health.

   1 Peter 2:24.

   He personally carried our sins in his body on the cross so that we can be dead to sin and live for what is right. By his wounds you are healed.

3. Jesus died to deliver me from the fear of death.

   Hebrews 2:14, 15 NLT

   Because God's children are human beings — made of flesh and blood — the son also became flesh and blood. For only as a human being could he die, and only by dying could he break the power of the devil, who had the power of death. Only in this way could he set free all who have lived their lives as slaves to the fear of dying.

4. Jesus' blood speaks forgiveness of sins for me.

   Hebrews 12:24 NLT
   You have come to Jesus, the one who mediates the new covenant between God and people, and to the sprinkled blood, which speaks of forgiveness instead of crying out for vengeance like the blood of Abel.

5. Jesus has delivered me from the power of sin.

   Romans 8:2
   And because you belong to him, the power of the life-giving Spirit has freed you from the power of sin that leads to death.
   Romans 6:7
   For when we died with Christ we were set free from the power of sin.

6. Jesus became poor that I might become rich.

   2 Corinthians 8:9 NLT
   You know the generous grace of our Lord Jesus Christ. Though he

was rich, yet for your sakes he became poor, so that by his poverty he could make you rich.

7. Jesus has redeemed me from any curse and has made me a blessing.

    Galatians 3:13, 14 NLT
    But Christ has rescued us from the curse pronounced by the law. When he was hung on the cross, he took upon himself the curse for our wrongdoing. For it is written in the scriptures, "Cursed is everyone who is hung on a tree." Through Christ Jesus, God has blessed the Gentiles with the same blessing he promised to Abraham, so that we who are believers might receive the promised Holy Spirit through faith.

8. Jesus took away any ordinances against me and defeated the devil for me.

    Colossians 2:13-15 NLT
    You were dead because of your sins and because your sinful nature was not yet cut away. Then God made you alive with Christ, for he forgave all our sins. He cancelled the record of the charges against us and took it away by nailing it to the cross. In this way, he disarmed the spiritual rulers and authorities. He shamed them publicly by his victory over them on the cross.

9. Jesus has set me free from any condemning charges.

    Romans 8:1, 2 NLT
    So now there is no condemnation for those who belong to Christ Jesus. And because you belong to him, the power of the life-giving Spirit has freed you from the power of sin that leads to death.

10. Jesus has made me a child of God.

    John 1:12 NLT
    But to all who believed him and accepted him, he gave the right to

become children of God.

11. Jesus has made me one with him.

1Corinthians 6:17 NLT

But the person who is joined to the Lord is one spirit with him.

12. Jesus has given me access to the Father.

Ephesians 1:5 NLT
God decided in advance to adopt us into his own family by bringing us to himself through Jesus Christ. This is what he wanted to do, and it gave him great pleasure.

13. Jesus has redeemed and forgiven my sins.

Colossians 1:14
In whom we have redemption through his blood, even the forgiveness of sins.

14. Jesus has made me complete.

Colossians 2:10 NLT
So you also are complete through your union with Christ, who is the head over every ruler and authority.

15. Jesus has set me free from condemning charges.

Romans 8:33, 34 NLT
Who dares accuse us whom God has chosen for his own? No one – for God himself has given us right standing with himself. Who then will condemn us? No one – for Christ Jesus died for us and was raised to life for us, and he is sitting in the place of honour at God's right hand, pleading for us.

16. Jesus has me on His side and I cannot be separated from him.

   Romans 8:35 NLT
   Can anything ever separate us from Christ's love? Does it mean he
   no longer loves us if we have trouble or calamity, or are persecuted,
   or hungry, or destitute, or in danger, or threatened with death?

17. Jesus has hidden me in Him.

   Colossians 3:3 NLT
   For you died to this life, and your real life is hidden with Christ in
   God.

18. Jesus has made me a citizen of heaven.

   Philippians 3:20 NLT
   But we are citizens of heaven, where the Lord Jesus Christ lives. And
   we are eagerly waiting for him to return as our Saviour.

19. Jesus has made me a personal witness of Him.

   Acts 1:8 NLT
   But you will receive power when the Holy Spirit comes upon you. And
   you will be my witnesses, telling people about me everywhere – in
   Jerusalem, throughout Judea, in Samaria, and to the ends of the earth.

20. Jesus has made my body God's temple.

   1 Corinthians 3:16 NLT
   Don't you realise that all of you together are the temple of God and
   that the Spirit of God lives in you?

21. Jesus has made me a new creature.

    1 Corinthians 5:17 NLT

    This means that anyone who belongs to Christ has become a new person. The old life is gone; a new life has begun!

22. Jesus has made me a minister of reconciliation.

    2 Corinthians 5:18 NLT

    And all of this is a gift from God, who brought us back to himself through Christ. And God has given us this task of reconciling people to him.

23. Jesus has made me God's fellow worker.

    2 Corinthians 6:1
    We then, as workers together with him, beseech you also that ye receive not the grace of God in vain.

24. Jesus has made me sit in heavenly places.

    Ephesians 2:6
    And hath raised us up together, and made us sit together in heavenly places in Christ Jesus:

25. Jesus has made me a workmanship of God.

    Ephesians 2:10
    For we are his workmanship, created in Christ Jesus unto good works, which God hath before ordained that we should walk in them.

26. Jesus has given me the boldness to come to God freely.

Ephesians 3:12 NLT
Because of Christ and our faith in him, we can now come boldly and confidently into God's presence.

27. Jesus has enabled me to do all things.

    Philippians 4:13 NLT
    For I can do everything through Christ, who gives me strength.

28. Jesus has made me an ambassador here on earth.

    2 Corinthians 5:20 NLT
    So we are Christ's ambassadors; God is making his appeal through us. We speak for Christ when we plead, "Come back to God!"

29. Jesus has given me the grace to live in triumph over sin and death.

    Romans 5:17 NLT

    For the sin of this one man, Adam, caused death to rule over many. But even greater is God's wonderful grace and his gift of righteousness, for all who receive it will live in triumph over sin and death through this one man, Jesus Christ.

30. Jesus has brought me peace with God.

    Romans 5:1 NLT
    Therefore, since we have been made right in God's sight by faith, we have peace with God because of what Jesus Christ our Lord has done for us.

    Ephesians 2:14 NLT
    For Christ himself has brought peace to us. He united Jews and Gentiles into one people when, in his own body on the cross, he broke down the wall of hostility that separated us.

31. Jesus has made me more than a conqueror.

    Romans 8:37

Nay, in all these things we are more than conquerors through him that loved us.

32. Jesus has brought me overwhelming victory.

Romans 8:37 NLT
No, despite all these things, overwhelming victory is ours through Christ, who loved us.

33. Jesus has brought me salvation.

Romans 10:9, 10 NLT
If you openly declare that Jesus is Lord and believe in your heart that God raised him from the dead, you will be saved. For it is by believing in your heart that you are made right with God, and it is by openly declaring your faith that you are saved.

CHAPTER 13
CHRIST-IN-ME BY GRACE CONFESSIONS

Being aware now that for the rest of our days
There's power that transforms in His mighty saving grace
So keep declaring and speaking it out
And when you do, believe and do not doubt

Before the year 2015 begun, my father in the faith, Daddy Evans Darko-Mensah, sent me the below grace confessions to declare them daily. I believe these confessions will be of a great blessing to you as you believe and declare them.

Colossians 1:26-27 NLT
This message was kept secret for centuries and generations past, but now it has been revealed to God's people.   For God wanted them to know that the RICHES and GLORY of Christ are for you Gentiles, too. And this is the secret: CHRIST LIVES IN YOU. This gives you assurance of sharing his glory.

Ephesians 2:4-6 NLT
But God is so rich in mercy, and HE LOVED US SO MUCH, that even though we were dead because of our sins, he gave us life when he raised Christ from the dead. (It is only by God's grace that you have been saved!) For he raised us from the dead along with Christ and seated us with him in the heavenly realms because we are UNITED WITH CHRIST JESUS.

Galatians 2:20 NLT
My old self has been crucified with Christ. It is no longer I who live,

89

but CHRIST LIVES IN ME. So I live in this earthly body by trusting in the Son of God, who loved me and gave himself for me.

1 Corinthians 15:10 NLT
But whatever I am now, it is all because God poured out his special favour (GRACE) on me — and not without results. For I have worked harder than any of the other apostles; YET IT WAS NOT I, but God who was working through me by HIS GRACE.

MY DAILY CONFESSION:

- I thank You Father, that You Love me so much that You have given me a New Life in Christ Jesus.

- I thank You Jesus, that You live in me Permanently by Your HOLY SPIRIT.

- By the Grace of God, I am what I am; yet Not I, but Christ in me.

Therefore:
- By the Grace of God, I am FULLY BLESSED; yet Not I, but Christ in me.

- By the Grace of God, I am LOVING; yet Not I, but Christ in me.

- By the Grace of God, I am JOYFUL; yet Not I, but Christ in me.

- By the Grace of God, I am PEACEFUL; yet Not I, but Christ in me.

- By the Grace of God, I am PATIENT; yet Not I, but Christ in me.

- By the Grace of God, I am KIND; yet Not I, but Christ in me.

- By the Grace of God, I am GOOD; yet Not I, but Christ in me.

- By the Grace of God, I am FAITHFUL; yet Not I, but Christ in me.

- By the Grace of God, I am GENTLE; yet Not I, but Christ in me.

- By the Grace of God, I am SELF-CONTROLLED; yet Not I, but Christ in me.

- By the Grace of God, I am OBEDIENT; yet Not I, but Christ in me.

- By the Grace of God, I am a SOUL WINNER; yet Not I, but Christ in me.

- By the Grace of God, I am WISE; yet Not I, but Christ in me.

- By the Grace of God, I am HEALTHY; yet Not I, but Christ in me.

- By the Grace of God, I am RICH; yet Not I, but Christ in me.

- By the Grace of God, I am INTELLIGENT; yet Not I, but Christ in me.

And so:

- By the Grace of God, I am THE BEST; yet Not I, but Christ in me.

- By the Grace of God, I have THE BEST; yet Not I, but Christ in me.

- By the Grace of God, I do THE BEST; yet Not I, but Christ in me.

- I give ALL the Glory to God, and my boast is in the LORD JESUS CHRIST.

  Amen.

Bibliography

1. Boateng, Kwasi. How to Enter the Throne Room of God through Worship. Accra: AGLC, 2013

2. "What is grace?" accessed via internet http://en.wikibooks.org/wiki/Hebrew_Roots/The_original_foundation/Grace

3. Munroe, Myles. Rediscovering the Kingdom, Destiny Image Publishers, USA, 2010

4. Price, Frederick K.C. Answered Prayer. Published by Charisma House, Florida, USA, 2011.

5. Sjogren, Steve. Servant Warfare (How Kindness conquers spiritual darkness). Michigan, 1996

6. Stanley, Andy. The Grace of God. Nashville: Thomas Nelson, 2010.

7. Cooke, Tony. Grace: The DNA of God. Tulsa, OK: Harrison House Publishers, © 2011